THE NEW WOMEN

♀ A

MOTIVE Anthology

on Women's Liberation

Edited by

Joanne Cooke,

Charlotte Bunch-Weeks,

and

Robin Morgan (Poetry Editor)

The

Bobbs-Merrill Company, Inc.

Indianapolis

New York

THE NEW

WOMEN——— ♀

The contents of this book previously appeared in the
March–April 1969 issue of *motive*, publication of the
Methodist Student Movement, with the exception of the following:

"The Demise of the Dancing Dog" by Cynthia Ozick,
which originally appeared in *Mademoiselle*

"Double Jeopardy" by Frances M. Beal

"A Broom of One's Own" by Charlotte Bunch-Weeks

"For a Brilliant Young Woman Who Lost Her Mind" by Rita Mae Brown

"Inside Outside" by Jean Tepperman

The editors gratefully acknowledge permission
to reprint the following:

from *Women: A Journal of Liberation*,
"My House in the Trees" by Joan Joesting
and "Birthright" by Margo Magid

from *The Rat*, "The Pill—Radio News 2/24/70"
by Marilyn Lowen Fletcher
and "To My Friend Miriam" by Martha Shelley

The Bobbs-Merrill Company, Inc.
A Subsidiary of Howard W. Sams & Co., Inc., Publishers
Indianapolis • Kansas City • New York

Library of Congress catalog card number 70-125895

Designed by Terry Reid

Printed in the United States of America

Contents

Contents

This book first appeared as a special double issue of *motive* magazine, March–April 1969, which seems rather mundane unless you know that *motive* is published by the Board of Education of the United Methodist Church, located in Nashville, Tennessee. "That issue," as it is now known, drew more letters, provoked more outrage and attracted more national attention than any other issue in the magazine's thirty-year history. It also put *motive* on the map for women all over the country, who began flooding the office with requests for extra copies for classes they were teaching, for conferences and seminars and study groups, for mothers and sisters, and "because mine keeps disappearing."

Most of the credit for this issue/book should go to Charlotte Bunch-Weeks. As one of the *motive* staff's favorite friends-and-relations, she knew we were planning a special issue on women, and she convinced the male editors that SOMEone should go to the women's liberation conference. It would be disastrous for *motive* to do a whole issue on women without at least mentioning the women's liberation movement, she said, and the conference would be a good place to observe it firsthand.

Right on. After the conference, it was clear to me as well as to Charlotte that the whole issue would have to be on the women's movement, still considered by the men of the staff to be a small, extreme lunatic fringe. In the face of two determined women, one of whom they had hired just six months earlier because she was "attractive, articulate and hip," the men finally agreed to let the two of us edit the issue. We called on Robin Morgan to select the poetry, and the whole thing became truly a "woman's issue."

As editors, we could see no reason to censor out the four-letter words. In fact, the words themselves were a political issue to us. The United Methodist Church found them a political issue, too. At that time, *motive* was operating under the implicit ultimatum that if any more of THOSE WORDS appeared, heads would roll. Charlotte and I assured the men that we would accept full re-

Preface

sponsibility, but the staff was still hierarchically organized then, and those higher up on the totem pole knew that they, and not two "foolish girls," would be held accountable. Still, it was "our baby" and the words stayed.

When the printers at the Methodist Publishing House refused to run the machines to print the issue, we knew we were really into something. Sure enough, no sooner had the issue come off the presses than phones started ringing, churchmen in business suits started coming to the office to demand an explanation, letters started pouring in, people started inviting me to speak to their church groups, and the issue started selling so fast we had to reprint it.

The letters were really incredible. Church people who had never heard of *motive* magazine had read that issue and were duly scandalized by the pornographic art, the dirty words and the suggestion that Eve was not inferior to Adam. We've included some of the best and most representative letters in the book, as much for fun as for your information. Almost all were addressed "Dear Sir" or "Gentlemen," and many went straight to the publisher for his "prompt attention to this matter." Sixty percent of the letters of congratulation were from women, while sixty percent of the letters of condemnation were from men.

When Bobbs-Merrill decided to do it as a book, Charlotte and I went back over the issue with an eye toward filling in the gaps we knew it left. Frances Beal agreed to let us use her article on black women, Robin selected some new poems, Charlotte wrote a survey of the development of the movement since the printing of the *motive* issue, and Sonia Jaffe Robbins held up Bobbs-Merrill's end by editing, polishing and prodding me with sisterly gentleness into doing this preface.

Power to the sisters, who are, after all, half of the people!

Joanne Cooke
August 1970

THE NEW WOMEN

♀ Here's to You, Mrs. Robinson: An Introduction

This book is about you and me. I don't know about you, but I'm probably pretty much like your sister or daughter or the girls you know. I wasn't born radical or found under a toadstool. My family is a perfectly normal American family—the kind that might produce an astronaut. Mother is an excellent cook and seamstress who has an R.N. and a beautiful laugh. I got my craving for magazines and my dimple from her. My father is a Methodist minister and a Lt. Col. chaplain in the Delaware Air National Guard who loves to sail. I got my crusading for social justice, my knack for getting involved in 99 causes at once and my double-jointed thumbs from him. My sister is a high school senior who's going to major in Home Ec. My brothers are a pre-ministerial college senior, a sports-and-art-loving high school junior and a nine-year-old Cub Scout.

I was a Girl Scout, myself, and I took piano, ballet, drama and swimming lessons, went to Scout and church camps, sang in choirs and choruses and folk groups, presidented the Methodist Youth Fellowship, helped edit the high school yearbook and worked in a department store. Two years ago I graduated from Randolph-Macon Woman's College, where I edited the newspaper and served on the College Council and the May Court, spending the summers as a waitress at the beach.

I'd been working for *motive* magazine for six months when I was sent, as token woman on the editorial staff, to the first national women's liberation conference, in Lake Villa, Illinois. Nothing has been the same since. Now every song on the radio, every magazine ad and TV commercial, every casual conversation, every store window is political. Not that I was that naive before, but politics didn't demand a change in life-style until I felt that I was being personally oppressed.

No one made more cracks about spending Thanksgiving weekend with a bunch of militant liberated women, no one thought it a bigger farce or dreaded it more than I. I was happy

By Joanne Cooke 

enough being a woman; what was wrong with *them?* Then they told me.

They talked about the Miss America contest. I had always resented beauty contests, but had never taken time to analyze why. I had considered campaigning editorially against the May Court at Randolph-Macon, but had talked myself out of it, only to have my motives confused by guilt upon being nominated for the dubious honor myself. These women clarified the whole thing. They *had* thought about it and had made a careful analysis. Their findings had, I think, surprised even them. All the evidence seemed to show that women in our society are still trained from infancy to entertain, to please and to serve—mainly men. Women are not yet raised to be just people—whole, fully participating individuals.

The women talked about everything that had ever bothered me, most of which I'd considered beyond discussion, having been told for twenty-two years that "that's the way it is." Here were two hundred women who had been meeting in groups in cities all over the U.S. and Canada to talk about the special problems women have.

What problems do women have that men don't? Why make women "another special interest group"? Why try to negotiate in the age-old battle of the sexes? What was so urgent that women would leave their families and friends at Thanksgiving to traipse off to some snowbound YMCA camp by a frozen lake to talk to *other women?*

So I listened. And I watched. The group was lily-white and seemed middle-class. The women ranged in age from about 17 to 60, and there were three or four small children running around. They talked about problems I'd known all my life. They filed the same complaints I'd heard at Brownie meetings, in the girls' room at high school dances, in dorm sessions, at bridge parties, in kitchen confabs, over back fences, at coffee breaks and cocktail parties. The only difference was that they were serious.

For the first time, I heard women discussing alternative ways of solving their problems. Not one woman said, "Well, that's how it is; what're you going to do?" Not one "Dear Abby" platitude. Not one woman apologized for complaints about her lot. Not only were they going to *do* something about it, they were supporting each other, committing themselves to helping each other in the process. Every woman was a sister and no sister's problem, idea or question was too trivial to be dealt with sympathetically.

No one was in charge. No one was an expert. Women took turns chairing the larger discussions. We took turns driving to pick up late arrivals, we volunteered to take shifts with the children, and we shared responsibility for the phone. Anyone with an idea or an interest to discuss was free to speak up or to set up a workshop.

Why should it be unusual for women to cooperate with and to support each other? Why should women be accustomed to competing with other women—for the attention of men?

When I saw that they were serious, that they were not going to be content to bitch but were already committed to changing their situation—*our* situation, when I heard what they'd already begun to do in cities all over the country, when I felt that I could trust them not to build up my hopes and then leave me flat, I accepted the fact that I was one of them.

You'd almost have to be a woman to understand. We each have an elaborate internal security system, carefully developed to protect us from those who would pry into our most secret doubts, dissatisfactions and questions and expose us as "masculine, lesbian, castrating, bitching communists." But when someone asks the right questions, without supplying the old and inadequate answers, the safe door swings open and lets us out, free and laughing in the fresh air.

No, that's not an exaggeration. All women know the old answers are inadequate. Anyone who has watched Shirley Temple's face when Captain January tells her she can't grow up to be a sailor 'cause she has to be a lady knows how totally frustrating the old answers are. Any woman who has cringed when told she was "smart, for a girl" or who has wanted to be complimented—just once—for her ideas rather than for the arrangement of her features or her figure knows how unsatisfactory the old answers are. Any woman who has tried to raise children alone—on a woman's salary—knows how little sense the old answers make.

What are the questions? Why do most expectant parents want a boy—at least, first? Why are little boys asked what they're going to be and little girls who their boyfriends are? Why do women have curfews when men don't? Why are we intimidated by the fashion and beauty industries? Why don't female executives have male secretaries? Where are all the female executives? Why do both women and men prefer male company? Why do we have to get married? Why do we have to have children? Why do women have the main responsibility for the care/feeding/education of the children men help them produce—even if both parents work? Why do we look to men for our definition, direction and strategy? Why do we have to live in pairs? Why do we pity/fear/ostracize lesbians? Why would anyone think we would want a cigarette of our own? Why do all the ads and commercials use women? Why do we spend all our time worrying about men when they spend most of theirs worrying about their work? Why do we not take our own work seriously? Why aren't women paid the same wages for doing the same work as men? Why do women distrust each other?

Why do we still believe that women are somehow different from men in ability, intelligence, talent and seriousness of purpose? If there are differences, why has no one asked "why" in the same tone that they have begun to ask why ghetto residents are stereotyped "shiftless and slow"? Why has no one dealt seriously with the ghettoization of women? Why are our problems considered insignificant or, at best, secondary? Why are we not organized to win and to protect our rights and interests? Whatever happened to our history? What would happen to society as we know it if we really worked at answers to some of these questions?

These are some of the questions around which a new movement for the liberation of women has grown. In this book some of the women involved in finding new answers by rephrasing old questions voice their concerns. The issue is primarily white and middle-class because it is mainly "Miss Ann" who has spoken out about woman-consciousness. So far, the women's movement is a priority mostly for white middle-class women with some "higher" education. In part, this reflects the secondary position of women's concerns, historically. We have always been led to believe that something else—anything else—was more important than our own welfare. However, if we really believe that no man is free unless all men are, then we must work for the freedom of all women as well. Black women, mill women, mountain women, mine women, Mexican-American women, farm women and factory women are beginning to realize this and to move also. Almost any Saturday night on the Grand Ole Opry, you can hear the Willis Brothers sing "Hertz Rent-a-Chick" shortly before or after Loretta Lynn sings "Your Good Girl's Gonna Go Bad" or "My Mistakes Are No Worse Than Yours Just Because I'm a Woman." It's everywhere, and it's growing.

It has become clear to me that "the woman thing," perhaps even more than "the black question," "the student problem," "the war," "the draft," or "the bomb"—demands a radical rethinking of our present concepts of human interaction and responsibility. To deal with the problems it raises demands basic changes in our assumptions about the organization of society—from the family to the state. (Is "Miss Ann" really free if she has to hire a black sister to tend her children and clean her house while she works? Who tends the maid's house and children? Where is *her* freedom?) How can we continue to support an economic, cultural and political system that oppresses not only its minorities but a clear 53% majority?

The four-letter words have been used intentionally. Our society has permitted certain words to become weapons, often used against women and taboo to them. We have to learn to be shocked, not at "bad" words but at the "bad" concepts behind their use. Look at some of them: "bastard" means son of an unmarried woman, "bitch" means female dog or complaining woman, "shit" is one of a myriad of words for excrement which "shocks" mothers, and "screw" and "fuck" mean not intercourse but its depersonalized version, involving the physical use of a woman one cares nothing about. These last two words are being used increasingly by women to refer to the male concept of impersonal sex. These words should all have been demythologized and disarmed long ago. And then there's the whole question of free speech. . . .

All this assumes brotherhood and sisterhood, with a radical call to mutual concern, involvement and commitment. It assumes working for justice and equality and dignity "on earth." And if fighting injustice, inequality and exploitation means a change basic enough to be called a revolution . . . Amen.

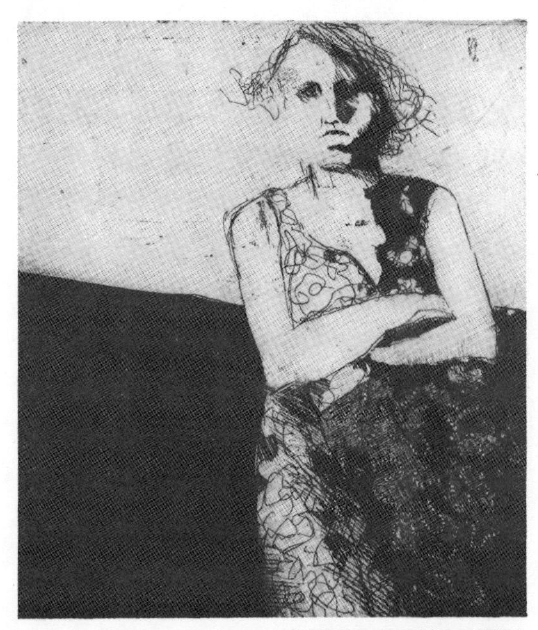

GOING DOWN HILL
Judith Stevens Sayfie

♀

The Demise of the Dancing Dog

Young women, . . . you are, in my opinion, disgracefully ignorant. You have never made a discovery of any importance. You have never shaken an empire or led an army into battle. The plays of Shakespeare are not by you, and you have never introduced a barbarous race to the blessings of civilization.
What is your excuse?

VIRGINIA WOOLF,
A ROOM OF ONE'S OWN

No comradely socialist legislation on woman's behalf could accomplish a millionth of what a bit more muscle tissue, gratuitously offered by nature, might do . . .

ELIZABETH HARDWICK,
A VIEW OF ONE'S OWN

I have just emerged from a year of Examining the Minds of the Young. It was a curious experience, like going into theatre after theatre in a single night, and catching bits of first acts only. What I saw of all those beginnings was extraordinary: they were all so similar. All the characters were exactly the same age, and most had equal limitations of imagination and aspiration.

"I have never in all my various travels seen but two sorts of people, and those very like one another; I mean men and women, who always have been, and ever will be, the same," wrote Lady Mary Wortley Montagu in the middle of the eighteenth century. Human nature is one.

By Cynthia Ozick

The vantage-point from which I came to these not unusual conclusions was not from reading the great philosophers, or even from reading Lady Mary—it was from a job. I was hired by a large urban university to teach English to freshmen: three classes of nearly a hundred young men and young women, all seventeen, some city-born, some suburban, some well off, some only scraping by, of every ethnic group and of every major religion but Hindu. Almost all were equipped with B high school averages; almost all were more illiterate than not; almost all possessed similar prejudices expressed in identical platitudes. They were identically uneducated, and the minds of the uneducated young women were identical with the minds of the uneducated men.

Now this last observation was the least surprising of all. I had never doubted that the human mind was a democratic whole—that it was androgynous, epicene, asexual: call it what you will. It had always seemed axiomatic to me that the minds of men and women were indistinguishable.

My students confirmed this axiom to the last degree. You could not tell the young men's papers from the young women's papers. They thought alike (badly); they wrote alike (gracelessly); and they believed alike (docilely). And what they all believed was this: that the minds of men and women are spectacularly unlike.

They believed that men write like men, and women like women; that men think like men, and women like women; that men believe like men, and women like women. And they were all identical in this belief.

Still, to teach at a university is not simply to teach; the teacher is a teacher among students, but he is also a teacher among teachers. He has colleagues, and to have colleagues is to have high exchanges, fruitful discourses, enlightening quarrels. Colleagues, unlike students, are not merely literate but breathtakingly literary; not merely educated but bent under the weight of multitudinous higher degrees; not merely informed but dazzingly knowledgeable; not merely unprejudiced but brilliantly questing.

And my colleagues believed exactly what my students believed.

My colleagues were, let it be noted, members of a Department of English in the prestige-college of an important university. I was, let it be revealed, the only woman instructor in that Department. Some years before, the college had been all male. Then the coeds were invited in, and now and then in their wake a woman was admitted, often reluctantly, to the faculty. I was in touch with novels, poetry, essays, enlarging meditations; but of "the world," as it turned out, I apparently knew little.

I came to the university in search of the world. I had just finished an enormous novel, the writing of which had taken many more years than any novel ought to take, and after so long a retreat my lust for the world was prodigious. I wanted Experience, I wanted to sleep under bridges—but finding that all the bridges had thickly trafficked cloverleafs under them, I came instead to the university. I came innocently. I had believed, through all those dark and hope-sickened years of writing, that it was myself ("myself"—whatever that means for each of us) who was doing the writing. In the university, among my colleagues, I discovered two essential points: (a) that it was a "woman" who had done the writing—not a mind—and that I was a "woman writer"; and (b) that I was now not a teacher, but a "woman teacher."

I was suspect from the beginning—more so among my colleagues than among my students. My students, after all, were accustomed to the idea of a "woman teacher," having recently been taught by several in high school. But my colleagues were long out of high school, and they distrusted me. I learned that I had no genuinely valid opinions, since every view I might hold was colored by my sex. If I said I didn't like Hemingway, I could have no *critical* justification, no *literary* reason; it was only because, being a woman, I obviously could not be sympathetic toward Hemingway's "masculine" subject-matter—the hunting, the fishing, the bullfighting, which no woman could adequately digest. It goes without saying that among my colleagues there were other Hemingway dissenters, but their reasons for disliking Hemingway, unlike mine, were not taken to be simply ovarian.

In fact, both my students and my colleagues were equal adherents of the Ovarian Theory of Literature, or, rather, its complement, the Testicular Theory. A recent camp-follower (I cannot call him a pioneer) of this explicit theory is, of course, Norman Mailer, who has attributed his own gift, and the literary gift in general, solely and directly to the possession of a specific pair of organs. One writes with these organs, Mailer has said in *Advertisements for Myself;* and I have always wondered with what shade of ink he manages to do it.

I recall my first encounter with the Ovarian Theory. My students had been assigned the reading of *Wise Blood,* the novella by Flannery O'Connor. Somewhere in the discussion I referred to the author as "she." The class stirred in astonishment; they had not imagined that "Flannery" could connote a woman, and this somehow put a different cast upon the narrative and their response to it. Now among my students there was a fine young woman, intelligent and experimental rather than conforming, one of my rare literates, herself an anomaly because she was enrolled in the overwhelmingly male college of Engineering. I knew that her mind usually sought beyond the commonplace—she wrote with the askew glance of the really inquisitive. Up went her hand.

"But I could *tell* she was a woman," she insisted. "Her sentences are a woman's sentences." I asked her what she meant and how she could tell. "Because they're sentimental," she said, "they're not concrete like a man's." I pointed out whole paragraphs, pages even, of unsentimental, so-called "tough" prose. "But she *sounds* like a woman—she has to sound that way because she is," said the future engineer, while I speculated whether her bridges and buildings would loom plainly as woman's work. Moreover, it rapidly developed that the whole class now declared that it too, even while ignorant of the author's sex, had nevertheless intuited all along that this was a woman's prose; it had to be, since Flannery was a she.

My second encounter with the idea of literature-as-physiology was odder yet. This time my interlocutor was a wonderfully gentle, deeply intellectual young fellow-teacher—he was going to *prove* what my freshmen had merely maintained. "But *of course* style is influenced by physical makeup," he began in his judicious graduate-assistant way. Here was his incontrovertible evidence: "Take Keats, right? Keats fighting tuberculosis at the end of his life. You don't suppose Keats' poetry was totally unaffected by his having had tuberculosis?" And he smiled with the flourish of a young man who has made an unanswerable point. "Ah, but *you* don't suppose," I put it to him cheerfully enough, "that being a woman is a *disease?*"

But comparing literary women with having a debilitating disease is the least of it. My colleague, after all, was a kindly sort, and stuck to human matters; he did not mention dogs. On the other hand, almost everyone remembers Dr. Johnson's remark upon hearing a woman preacher—she reminded him, he said, of a dog dancing on its hind legs; one marvels not at how well it is done, but that it is done at all. That was two centuries ago; wise Lady Mary was Johnson's contemporary. Two centuries, and the world of letters has not been altered by a syllable, unless you regard the switch from dogs to disease as a rudimentary advance. Perhaps it is. We have advanced so far that the dullest as well as the best of freshmen can scarcely be distinguished from Dr. Johnson, except by a bark.

And our own Dr. Johnson—I leave you to guess his name—hoping to insult a rival writer, announces that the rival "reminds me of nothing so much as a woman writer."

Consider, in this vein, the habits of reviewers. I think I can say in good conscience that I have never—repeat, *never*—read a review of a novel or, especially, of a collection of poetry by a woman which did not include somewhere in its columns a gratuitous allusion to the writer's sex and its supposed effects. The Ovarian Theory of Literature is the property of all society, not merely of freshmen and poor Ph.D. lackeys: you will find it in all the best periodicals, even the most highbrow.

Reviewers must take merit as their point of concentration, not the flap of skirts, not the glibbest of literary canards. Still, the canards are, in their way, great fun, being as flexible and fragile as other toys. A collection of canards is bound to be a gaggle of contradictions. When, for instance, my bright engineering student identified Flannery O'Connor as "sentimental," she was squarely in one-half of a diluvial, though bifurcated, tradition. Within this tradition there are two hoary views of woman. One: she is sentimental, imprecise, irrational, overemotional, impatient, unperseveringly flighty, whimsical, impulsive, unreliable, unmechanical, not given to practicality, perilously vague, and so on. In this view she is always contrasted with man, who is, on the other hand, unsentimental, exact, rational, controlled, patient, hard-headed, mechanically gifted, a meeter of payrolls, firm of purpose, wary of impulse, anything but a dreamer.

Description Number One accounts for why, throughout her history, she has been a leader neither of empires nor of trades nor of armies. But it is also declared that, her nature having failed her in the practical world, she cannot succeed in the world of invention either: she is unequipped, for example, for poetry, in that (here is Description Number Two) she is above all pragmatic, sensible and unsentimental, unvisionary, unadventurous, empirical, conservative, down-to-earth, unspontaneous, perseveringly patient and thus good at the minutiae of mechanical and manipulative tasks, and essentially unimaginative. In short, she will wander too much or she will wander not at all. She is either too emotional or she is not emotional enough. She is either too spontaneous or she is not spontaneous enough. She is either too sensitive (that is why she cannot be president of General Motors) or she is not sensitive enough (that is why she will never write *King Lear*).

But none of this is to imply that woman is damned, and damned from every direction. Not at all. The fact is that woman *qua* woman is more often celebrated. If she cannot hear the Muse, says Robert Graves, what does it matter? She *is* the Muse. *Man Does, Woman Is,* is the title of Graves' most recent collection of poetry. If we are expected to conclude from this that woman is an It rather than a Thou, why deplore it? The Parthenon, too, is beautiful, passive, inspiring. Who would long to *build* it, if one can *be* it?

And even this is unfair, for it is simultaneously true that woman is frequently praised as the more "creative" sex. She does not need to make poems, it is argued, she has no drive to make poems, because she is privileged to make babies. A pregnancy is as fulfilling as, say, Yeats' *Sailing to Byzantium*. Here is an interesting idea worth examination. To begin with, we would have to know what it cost Yeats—I am speaking physically—to wring out a poem of genius. Perhaps we cannot know this. The writing of great and visionary literature is not a common experience, and is not readily explorable. Yeats himself spoke of the poet living amid whirlwinds. Virginia Woolf, a writer of a kind of prose very near poetry in tone and aspiration, was racked in the heat of composition by seizures of profoundly tormenting headaches. Isaac Babel called himself a "galley slave." Conrad was in a frenzy for weeks on end—"I turn in this vicious circle and the work itself becomes like the work in a treadmill—a thing without joy—a punishing task. . . . I am at it day after day, and I want all day, every minute of a day, to produce a beggarly tale of words or perhaps to produce nothing at all. . . . One's will becomes the slave of hallucinations, responds only to shadowy impulses, waits on imagination alone." Dostoyevsky said plainly: *"I worked and was tortured."*

That is what "creativity" is. Is a pregnancy like that? The fact is, given health, the condition of pregnancy is—in the consciousness—very nearly like the condition of non-pregnancy. It is insulting to a poet to compare his titanic and agonized strivings with the so-called "creativity" of child-bearing, where—consciously—nothing happens. One does not will the development of the foetus; one can be as dull or as active, as bored or as intense, as one pleases—anything else is mere self-absorption and daydreams: the process itself is as involuntary and as unaware as the beating of one's own heart. Of course, it is a miracle that one's heart goes on beating, that the foetus goes on growing—but it is not a human miracle, it is Nature's miracle.

To call a child a poem may be a pretty metaphor, but it is a slur on the labor of art. Literature cannot be equated with physiology, and woman through her reproductive system alone is no more a creative artist than was Joyce by virtue of his kidneys alone, or James by virtue of his teeth (which, by the way, were troublesome). A poem emerges from a mind, and mind is, so far as our present knowledge takes us, an unknowable abstraction. Perhaps it is a compliment to a woman of no gifts to say of her in compensation, "Ah, well, but she has made a child." But that is a cheap and slippery mythology, and a misleading one.

All this is, one would think, almost stupefyingly obvious. It is embarrassing, it is humiliating, to be so obvious about the quality either of literature or of woman. She, at any rate, is not a Muse, nor is she on the strength of her womb alone an artist. She is—how stupidly obvious!—a person. She can be an artist if she was born talented. She can be a Muse if she inspires a poet, but she, too (if she was born talented), can find her own Muse in another person. Mme. de Sevigne's Muse was her daughter, and what male Muse it was who inspired Emily Bronte's Heathcliff, history continues to conjecture. The Muse —*pace* Robert Graves—has no settled sex or form, and can appear in the shape of a tree (cf. *Howards End*) or a city (the Paris of *The Ambassadors*) or even—think of Proust!—a cookie.

Yet in our culture, in our country, much is not obvious. With respect to woman and with respect to literature, ours is among the most backward areas on earth. It is true that woman has had the vote for forty-five years, and she has begun to enter most professions, though often without an invitation. We are far past the grievances Virginia Woolf grappled with in *A Room of One's Own* and *Three Guineas*—books which are still sneered at as "feminist." In 1929, when Virginia Woolf visited Oxford (or was it Cambridge? she is too sly to say which), she was chased off a lawn forbidden to the feet of women. By then, of course, our colleges were already full of coeds, though not so full as now. And yet the question of justification remains.

Only a few months ago, in my own college, a startling debate was held—"Should a Woman Receive a College Education?" The audience was immense, but the debaters were only three: an instructor in Anthropology (female), a professor of History (male), and a fiercely bearded professor of Psychology (ostentatiously male). According to the unironic conventions of chivalry, the anthropologist spoke first. She spoke of opportunities and of problems. She spoke of living wholly and well. She did not ignore the necessities and difficulties of housekeeping and child-rearing; she spoke of the relations of parents, children, and work-in-the-world; she talked extensively about nursery-schools.

She took as her premise not merely that a woman ought to be fully educated, but that her education should be fully used in society. She was reasoned and reasonable; she had a point of view. Perhaps it was a controversial point of view, perhaps not—her listeners never had the chance of a serious evaluation. Her point of view was never assailed or refuted. It was overlooked. She spoke—against mysterious whispered cackles in the audience—and sat. Then up rose the laughing psychologist, and cracked jokes through his beard. Then up rose the laughing historian, and cracked jokes through his field—I especially remember one about the despotism of Catherine the Great: "That's what happens when a woman gets emancipated." Laughter from all sides.

Were the historian and the psychologist laughing at the absurdity of the topic the callow students' committee had selected for debate? An absurd topic—it deserves to be laughed out of court, and surely that is exactly what is happening, for here in the audience are all these coeds, censuring and contradicting by their very presence the outrageous question. Yet look again: the coeds are laughing, too. Everyone is laughing the laughter of mockery. They are not laughing at the absurdly callow topic. They are laughing at the buffoonery of the historian and the psychologist, who are themselves laughing at the subject of the topic: the whole huge room, packed to the very doors and beyond with mocking boys and girls, is laughing at the futility of an educated woman. *She* is the absurdity.

The idea of an educated woman is not yet taken seriously in American universities. She is not chased off the campus, she is even welcomed there—but she is not taken seriously as a student, and she will not be welcomed if she hopes to return as a serious lifelong scholar. Nor will she be welcomed afterward in the "world." A law firm may hire her, but it will hide her in its rear research offices, away from the eyes of clients. The lower schools will receive her, as they always have, for she is their bulwark; their bulwark, but not their principal, who is a man. We have seen her crawling like Griselda through the long ordeal of medicine: she is almost always bound to be a pediatrician, for it is in her nature to "work with children."

I will not forget the appalling laughter of the two mocking debaters. But it was not so appalling as the laughter of the young men and the young women in the audience. In the laughter of the historian and the psychologist I heard the fussy cry—a cry of violated venerable decorum, no doubt—of the beadle who chased Virginia Woolf off the grass in 1929. But what of that youthful mockery? It was hideous; it showed something ugly and self-shaming about the nature of our society and the nature of our education—and by "our education" I do not mean the colleges, I mean the kindergartens, I mean the living-rooms at home, I mean the fathers and the mothers, the men and the women.

In this country the women, by and large, are at home. Why? Well, plainly because they belong there. They are there to rear the children, and if they have a whole lot of children, there will usually be a helpless baby. The mother is at home to take care of the helpless baby. That is right and reasonable. Everyone agrees—Nature agrees, the father agrees, society agrees.

Society agrees? That is very interesting. That, too, is an idea worth examination. It is very useful for society to have the mother at home. It keeps her out of the way. If, say, she stopped at only two children—but if she stopped at only two, she would be in danger of reducing the birthrate, which now rivals India's—if she stopped at two, those two might be half-grown, and safely shut up in a school building most of the day, by the time she is thirty-five. And if she were thirty-five—a young, healthy, able, educated thirty-five—with no helpless baby to keep her at home, and most of the day free, what would she do?

Society shudders at the possibility: she might want to get a job. But that would never do. Why, if you counted up all the young, healthy, able, educated, free women of thirty-five, it might come to nearly half the population! And, as things stand now, there are not even enough jobs for the other half of the population, the truly bread-winning half. And what about all those three-quarters-grown persons we call adolescents? Society shudders at them, too: the economy is an inn with no room for adolescents and women. But if it will not allow adolescents and women to share in its work (how can it? so much of the work is done by machines), society must at least provide something else to keep the adolescents and women occupied, if only artificially. So, out of the largesse of its infinitely adaptable lap, it gives women knitting and adolescents transistor radios to dance to. (And for the adolescents of even mediocre capacities—here, there is no discrimination by sex—it comes up with colleges, and fraudulent debates, and more dancing.)

Society provides a complete—and in essence custodial—culture for each group it is forced to keep out of the way. It is a culture of busywork and make-believe and distraction. Society is very clever, and always has been. Once upon a time, before machines, women and adolescents *were* needed and used to the last degree in the economy. Women were not educated because an unautomated house requires a work-horse to maintain it, and a woman who cannot read or write is somehow better at hauling water in from the pump than one who can. (Why this should be, only the experience of society can explain.) But now society—so long as we fail to renovate it—can furnish work for only a quarter of the population, and so the rest must be lured into thinking it is performing a job when it is really not doing anything beyond breathing.

That is why there are in our society separate minority cultures for adolescents and for women. Each has its own set of opinions, prejudices, tastes, values, and—do not underestimate this last—magazines. You and I are here concerned only with the culture of women. Society, remember, is above men and women; it acts *in* men and women. So you must not make the mistake of thinking that the culture of women is the conspiracy of men. Not in the least. That is an old-fashioned, bluestocking view of the matter, and it is erroneous. The culture of women is believed in by both men and women, and it is the conspiracy of neither, because it is the creature neither of men alone, nor of women alone, but of society itself—that autonomous, cunning, insensitive sibling of history.

The culture of women consists of many, many things—products as well as attitudes, but attitudes mostly. The attitudes generate the products, and the products utilize the attitudes. The most overriding attitude is summed up in a cult-word: "Home." (Notice that builders do not sell houses, they sell "homes"—a case of attitude and product coalescing.) But what does "Home" mean? It means curtains, rugs, furniture, a boiler in the cellar, magazines with dress patterns and recipes and articles full of adulterated Freud, a dog, a box of cereal-bones for the dog, a kitchen floor that conscience insists must be periodically waxed, and so forth: but mostly, of course, it means "Children." And "Children" are not regarded as incomplete or new persons, as unformed destinies, as embryo participants in the society—above all, they are not regarded simply as *children:* they are a make-believe entity in themselves, a symbol of need and achievement, just as the dog-biscuits (not real bones) are a make-believe entity in themselves (does the dog think they are real?). "Children" as a concept have, in their present incarnation, a definite function, which is to bolster the whole airy system of make-believe. "Children" are there to justify "Home"; and "Home" is there to justify a third phantom entity—the heroine of the fairytale, also an invention and an abstraction, the "Homemaker."

This is our "problem"—the problem of a majority's giving its credence and its loyalty to a daydream. And it is a bigger problem than any other we know of in this country, for the plain and terrifying reason that we do not even consider it to be a problem. Whenever the cliché-question is put, "What is the Number One problem in America today?" the cliché-answer comes: "Civil rights—the Negro Revolution." Scarcely. The solution to *that* problem is *there*—we have only to catch up to it, and with all our might. If the debate at my college had dealt with civil rights, it would have been serious and passionate and argumentative. We had a Vietnam teach-in: *it* was serious and passionate and argumentative. But no one will be serious and passionate, and certainly no one will be argumentative, concerning attitudes about and of women. Once a problem has been articulated, the answer is implicit; the answer is already fated. But this problem is never articulated; there is no answer, because no one asks the question. It is a question that has not yet found its Malcolm. Its substance is, on every level, the stuff of primitive buffoonery.

Well, what *is* the question? Who will formulate it? "Feminists" will not, because it is not a feminist question. It is not a group question or a special-interest question or a conspiratorial question. It is a humanist question. (And yet note how questions that long ago began as purely "feminist," such as birth control with Margaret Sanger, eventually become the foremost and profoundest of humanistic concerns. One has only to read Julian Huxley's essays on evolution in relation to population expansion to grasp this.) Nor will documents formulate it—I am thinking of a recent very popular document, a tract called *The Feminine Mystique*. It was, as tracts go, a suberb one, but tracts give answers, somewhat mechanically, and here the question has not yet been put. Besides, it is poets, and never sociologists (still less those even more amorphous persons called "social thinkers"), who are traditionally the formulators and articulators of those seminal questions to which the majority is deaf: the prophets were artists and not lecturers, and so were the composers of our spirituals.

Virginia Woolf is the artist-pioneer, the Margaret-Sanger-as-bard, so to speak, of this social question. Among artists, she has no successor. Not until art has seized and possessed and assimilated this question will it begin to interest the scientist-humanists.

But what are the components of the question? Here they are: no great female architects, painters, playwrights, sailors, bridge-builders, jurists, captains, composers, etc., etc.

Here I think of a curious analogy. Say what you will about the gifted Jews, they have never, up until times so recent that they scarcely begin to count, been plastic artists. Where is the Jewish Michelangelo, the Jewish Rembrandt, the Jewish Rodin? He has never come into being. Why? Have oppression and persecution erased the possibility of his existence? Hardly. Oppression and persecution often tend to reinforce gifts; to proscribe is more effective than to prescribe. Where, then, *is* the Jewish

Michelangelo? Is it possible that a whole people cannot produce a single painter? And not merely a single painter of note, but a single painter *at all?* Well, there *have* been artists among the Jews—artisans, we should more likely call them, decorators of trivial ceremonial objects, a wine-cup here, a scroll-cover there. Talented a bit, but nothing great. They never tried their hand at wood or stone or paint. "Thou shalt have no graven images"—the Second Commandment—prevented them. And it is not until a very, very little while ago, under the influence of a movement called "Emancipation," or "Enlightenment," that we begin to see creeping in a Chagall, a Modigliani, an Epstein, who have ceased to believe that art insults the Unity of God. It will be a long, long time before the Jews have their Michelangelo. Before a "David" can happen, a thousand naked Apollos must be hewn. (And Apollo *did* insult the Unity of God.) There must be a readied ground, a preparation—in short, a relevant living culture to frame the event.

The same, I think, with our problem. Gifts and brains are not transmitted, like hemophilia, from the immune sex to the susceptible sex. Genius is the property of both sexes and all nations alike. That is the humanist view. The Jews have had no artists not because they have had no genius for art, but because their image of themselves as a culture inhibited the exercise of the latent gift. And all those non-existent female Newtons and Bachs and Leonardos and Shakespeares—they have had no more chance of leaping from the prison of their societal fates than any Greek slave, or a nomad's child in Yemen today.

The emancipation of women is spectacularly new. As with what we now call the Black Revolution, it is clear that emancipation does not instantly result in achievement. Enlightenment must follow. And the enlightenment has, for women, and especially by women, not yet occurred.

It has not yet occurred even at the most expressive point of all—in the universities. It is the function of a liberal university not to give right answers, but to ask right questions. And the ultimate humanist question, as we have seen, has not yet been expressed (my students had never in all their lives heard it put); the components of the unrealized question, as we have seen, are the experiences and needs and omissions and premises of a culture. A culture can have a seemingly unchanging premise, and then suddenly it will change; hence, among the Jews, Chagall and Modigliani and Epstein; hence, in literature, the early epistolary artists—Mme. de Sevigne and Lady Mary—and then, close on their heels, the genius novelists, Jane and George. Literature was the first to begin it, since literature could be pursued privately and at home.

Cultivation precedes fruition. Perhaps we cannot have our great women architects, painters, playwrights, sailors, bridge-builders, jurists, captains, composers, and so forth, until we have run-of-the-mill women in these roles, until all that is a commonplace—until, in short, women enter into the central stream of mankind's activities, until woman-as-person becomes as flat and unremarked a tradition as man-as-person. Reproduction, trick it out as you will in this or that myth, is still only reproduction, a natural and necessary biological function, and biology, however fancied up with tribal significance and mystical implication, is not enough. Unless you are on the extreme verge of death, it is never enough just to keep on breathing.

Even woman's differing muscular capacity—much is made of this, unsurprisingly—is, in the age of the comprehensive machine, an obstacle to almost no pursuit. The machine widens experience for everyone, and equalizes the physical endurance of men and women. A long journey is no longer a matter of muscle, but of jet schedules. Presumably, it will become harder and harder to maintain that novelists who are women are condemned to a narrower focus than that of men because their lives are perforce narrower.

The question is, then, I believe, a question touching at least peripherally on art. Not merely literary art, but all the human arts, including those we call science. And I have ventured that the question must be formulated as a humanistic issue, not a sectarian one, not a divisive one. Art must belong to all human beings, not alone to a traditionally privileged segment; every endeavor, every passion, must be available to the susceptible adult, without the intervention of myth or canard.

Woman will cease solely to be man's Muse—an It (as she is,

curiously, for writers as disparate as Graves and Mailer, as she was for Freud)—and will acquire Muses of her own when she herself ceases to be bemused with gaudy daydreams and romances—with lies reinforcing lies—about her own nature. She limits—she self-limits—her aspirations and her expectations. She joins the general mockery at her possibilities. I have heard her laughing at herself as though she were a dancing dog. You have seen her regard her life as a disease to be constantly tended and pacified. She does not yet really believe that she is herself accessible to poetry or science: she wills these into her sons, but not into her daughters. She surrounds herself with the devices and manipulations of an identity that is not an identity. Without protest she permits the intractable momentum of society to keep her from its worthinesses and larger adventures, from its expressive labor. She lives among us like a docile captive; a consuming object; an accomplice; an It. She has been successfully persuaded to work for and at her own imprisonment.

If one were to bow to the tempting idea that her role has come about through a conspiracy (as it could not have, for custom is no plot), it would appear as though it were a conspiracy of sluggish women, and never of excluding men. The fervor and energies of the women who are not lazy, those rare activist personalities who feel the call of a Cause, are thrown pragmatically into the defense of that easy and comfortable role; the barricades of the pleasant prison are manned—no, womaned—by the inmates themselves, to prevent the rebels from breaking out.

But the rebels are few.

That is because, among us, no one rebels, no one protests, no one wants to renovate or liberate, no one asks any fundamental questions. We have, alas, the doubtful habit of reverence. Above all we respect things-as-they-are. If we want to step on the moon, it is not to explore an unknown surface or to divine a new era, but to bolster ourselves at home, among the old home rivals; there is more preening than science in that venture, less boldness than bravado. We are so placid that the smallest tremor of objection to anything at all is taken as a full-scale revolution: a bunch of college students sit down, and university presidents at commencements all over the country begin *en masse* to chirp out alarmed and startled strictures on the subject of rashness, failing discipline, the threat to civil peace. Should anyone speak up in favor of the obvious, it is taken as a symptom of the influence of the left, the right, the pink, the black, the hippie. An idea for its own sake—especially an obvious idea—has no respectability.

Among my last year's students—let us come back to *them,* for they are our societal prototypes—all of this was depressingly plain. That is why they could not write intelligibly—no one had ever mentioned the relevance of writing to thinking, and thinking had never been encouraged or induced in them. By "thinking" I mean, of course, not the simple ability to make equations come out right, but the devotion to speculation on that frail but obsessive distraction known as the human condition. My students—male and female—did not need to speculate on what goals are proper to the full life; male and female, they already knew their goals. And their goals were identical. They all wanted to settle down into a perpetual and phantom coziness. They were all at heart sentimentalists—and sentimentalists, Yeats said, are persons "who believe in money, in position, in a marriage bell, and whose understanding of happiness is to be so busy whether at work or play, that all is forgotten but the momentary aim." Accordingly, they had all opted, long ago, perhaps at birth, for the domestic life, the enclosed life, the constricted life—the life, in brief, of the daydream, into which the obvious must not be permitted to thrust its scary beams.

By the "obvious" I mean, once again, the gifts and teachings and life-illuminations of art. The methods of art are variegated, flexible, abstruse, and often enough mysterious. But the burden of art is obvious: here is the world, here are human beings, here is childhood, here is struggle, here is hate, here is old age, here is death. None of these is a fantasy, a romance, or a sentiment, none is an imagining; all are obvious. A culture which does not allow itself to look clearly at the obvious through the universal accessibility of art is a culture of tragic delusion, hardly viable; it will make room for a system of fantasy Offices on the one hand,

and a system of fantasy Homes on the other, but it will forget that the earth lies beneath all.

Such a culture will turn out role-playing stereotypes (the hideousness of the phrase is appropriate to the concept) instead of human beings. It will shut the children away from half the population. It will shut aspiration away from half the population. It will glut its colleges with young people enduringly maimed by illusions learned early and kept late. It will sup on make-believe. But a humanistic society—you and I do not live in one—is one in which a voice is heard: "Come," it says, "here is a world requiring architects, painters, playwrights, sailors, bridge-builders, jurists, captains, composers, discoverers, and a thousand things besides, all real and all obvious. Partake," it says, "live."

Is it a man's voice or a woman's voice? Students, colleagues, listen again; it is two voices. "How obvious," you will one day reply, and if you laugh, it will be at the quaint folly of obsolete custom, which once failed to harness the obvious; it will not be at a dancing dog.

Revolutionary Letter
By Diane Di Prima

#1

I have just realized that the stakes are myself
I have no other
ransom money, nothing to break or barter but my life
my spirit measured out, in bits, spread over
the roulette table, I recoup what I can
nothing else to shove under the nose of the maitre de jeu
nothing to thrust out the window, no white flag
this flesh all I have to offer, to make the play with
this immediate head, what it comes up with, my move
as we slither over this board, stepping always
(we hope) between the lines

Inside Outside
By Jean Tepperman

I want to be very clear.
rough careful
a broad-boned face
brown curly hair
eyes and a forehead
heavy leg bones
very clear
sorting out
exercise
talking
making people laugh
laughing
walking on the street
eating cheese
orange
salt
dry grass
brown dirt warm sun
cities typewriters
Looking is easier for me
than listening.
Why is that?
Wondering.

A girl is in a mirror.
Lady chick broad skirt bird
young thing slip of a thing
in a mirror.
A man smiles.
He moves, he lights a cigarette
He stands up
he moves closer, smiling.
A girl in a mirror
space light prisms

small
smaller
little, pretty, light
a blue skirt
delicate smaller.
The top of her head
fits easily under the table.
She looks up
a man smiles
hand on her head.
Light, floating
far away
mirror echoes
music fading
breath wind
going away
A girl in a mirror
smiling pretty
very small.

I can't find it
it's lost
it doesn't fit
tight, can't breathe
stay, go away
inside outside
where is it?

He didn't mean to
he didn't mean to
Did he mean to?
Get him out of here.
Leave the room
blank mirror

sleep
breathe
walk
It's all right
it's all right.

I want to be very clear.
I look at my foot.
My foot looks at me.
We are friends again.
A person might say hello.
My foot and I together
might say hello back.
Walking slow
breathing
I would like
to be very clear
about my arm.
I would like to feel
that the top of my head
will not suddenly begin pressing down.
A man smiles
he moves, he stands up
he moves closer, smiling.
I want to be very clear about this.

LITHOGRAPH: FLIGHT
Betty La Duke

♀

The Restless Eagles: Women's Liberation 1969

Like the rumble of guns
From afar . . .
I am tired of mating and meandering
I want the yellow canyons of desire
I will be no docile thing—
But a restless eagle in space

BLANCHE SHOEMAKER WAGSTAFF,
ATAVISM (1929)

". . . 'and the nearer we got to the church, the madder I was; and now,' says she, 'do you reckon after all I'd been through that mornin', and dinner ahead of me to git, and the children to look after all the evenin', do you reckon that I felt like settin' up there and singin' "Welcome, sweet day of rest"?' Says she, 'I ain't seen any day o' rest since the day I married Sam, and I don't expect to see any till the day I die; and if Parson Page wants that hymn sung, let him git up a choir of old maids and old bachelors, for they're the only people that ever see any rest Sunday or any other day.' "

ELIZA CALVERT HALL,
AUNT JANE OF KENTUCKY (1907)

Women's liberation is not a new movement, but rather a rebirth of insurgency. It is the latest wave in the unfinished revolution waged by women in America throughout the ages of their oppression.

By Marlene Dixon 

Margaret Fuller wrote in 1845, in *Woman in the Nineteenth Century,* what is regrettably a most contemporary document. In her introduction to the book, she wrote:

I have aimed to show that no age was left entirely without a witness of the equality of the sexes in function, duty and hope. Also that, when there was unwillingness or ignorance, which prevented this being acted upon, women had not the less power for their want of light and noble freedom. But it was power which hurt alike them and those against whom they made use of the arms of the servile—cunning, blandishment, and unreasonable emotion.

I believe that, at present, women are the best helpers of one another. Let them think; let them act; till they know what they need. We ask of men to remove arbitrary barriers. Some would like to do more. But I believe it needs that Woman show herself in her native dignity, to teach them how to aid her; their minds are so encumbered by tradition.

Women might indeed take pride in the history of their freedom struggle—if they knew about that history! That women (and men) are ignorant of the history of women's liberation movements is no accident. It is part of the whole fabric of oppression of women whose history has been rewritten into a bizarre comic opera of bluestockings and suffragettes. The distortion of women's history has made women ashamed and afraid of being called unfeminine and grotesque. This fear has kept women from voicing their discontent and demanding their rights to a full and free life of their own.

History is not the only collaborator in perpetuating the social myths which justify the continued subjugation of women. Psychiatry, for example, portrays women chiefly as sexual beings, suitable only for childbearing, and doomed to *frustration* if their lives are not given over wholly to *nurturance*. These translations of the "common wisdom" into scientific law perpetuate the myth of the subservient role of women. Yet, as psychologist Naomi Weisstein emphasizes in another article in this issue, such arguments are wrong: "There isn't the tiniest shred of evidence that these (psychiatric) fantasies of servitude and childish dependence have anything to do with woman's true potential."

Sociology is also guilty of translating the subservient social role of women into "scientific law." Sociologists argue that the role of women cannot change because the division of labor *requires* sex-role differentiation. In other words, what *has* been, *must* be. Yet when the sociologist happens to be a woman, different conclusions must be reached. Mrs. Alice Rossi, for example, argues:

> There is no overt antifeminism in our society (in 1964), not because sex equality has been achieved, but because there is practically no feminist spark left among American women. When I ask the brightest of my women college students about their future study and work plans, they either have none because they are getting married in a few months, or they show clearly that they have lowered their aspirations from professional and research fields that excited them as freshmen, to concentrate as juniors on more practical fields far below their abilities. Young women seem increasingly uncommitted to anything beyond early marriage, motherhood and a suburban house. There are few Nora's in contemporary American society because women have deluded themselves that the doll's house is large enough to find complete personal fulfillment within it.[1]

Mrs. Rossi explains the decline in the feminist movement by showing that changes in the legal code or obtaining the right to vote is no guarantee that changes in patterns of exploitation and discrimination will follow. Legal changes are often hollow victories.

Feminism became nonexistent during the affluent and politically conservative years following World War II. Just recall those grotesque Hollywood movies of the '50's: brilliant woman gives up all to marry Mr. Clean: a not very subtle variant on the happy themes of "a woman's place is in the home," "keep her barefoot and pregnant," and "a woman's brains are between her legs."

With grease and with grime from corner to center
Forever at war and forever alert
No rest for a day lest the enemy enter
I spend my whole life in a struggle with dirt

[1] Alice Rossi, "Equality Between the Sexes: An Immodest Proposal," *The Women in America,* Houghton Mifflin, 1965.

Alas! 'Twas no dream; ahead I behold it,
I see I am helpless my fate to avert
She lay down her broom, her apron she folded
She lay down and died and was buried in dirt.

"THE HOUSEWIFE'S LAMENT,"
AMERICAN FOLKSONG

There were 44 million unpaid domestic workers in the U.S. in 1965: married women keeping house. In an average month in 1962, there were 23 million women at work, of whom 17 million were full-time workers. Most of the jobs that women hold are in low-pay categories. In 1960, for example, there were 7 million women clerical workers and only 431 geologists. In 1961 the earnings of women working full time averaged only about 60 per cent of those of men working full time: women are paid less for the same work. Studies made in 1960 showed area averages of women bank-tellers with less than five years of experience running typically $5–15 a week less than the averages of men with the same number of years of experience. Differences ranged from 9 to 49 cents an hour between the averages of men and women in the same power laundry occupations in a number of metropolitan areas. (*American Women,* The Report of the President's Commission on the Status of Women and Other Publications of the Commission, Scribner's, 1965).

Other aspects of the economic exploitation of women and discrimination against them must be cited: Negro women constitute the largest minority in the United States, and are the lowest paid and the most disadvantaged group in the labor force. The median annual wage of white women is less than that of black men. In 1960, nonwhite males earned $3,075; white females, $2,537. Lowest of all are the nonwhite females: $1,276. Yet the black woman often earns more than her husband, and sometimes is the only wage earner in the family. Finally, women are educationally disadvantaged by early marriage: less than half of all women 25 years of age and over are high school graduates. There are almost 4 million adult women with less than five years of schooling; 11.5 million women have not completed high school; only one in three of the bachelor's and master's degrees conferred by universities and colleges goes to women, and only one in ten of the Ph.D.'s. "These ratios represent a significant decrease since the 1930's, when two out of five bachelor's and master's degrees and one out of seven Ph.D.'s were earned by women,"[2] observes Esther Peterson.

Why have women passively accepted the massive economic and social exploitation of their position in American life? It is because they are taught at home and at school that they are secondary to men, that their lives must be lived through their husbands, their futures experienced through their children. They occupy the status of appendages to others' lives. David McClelland emphasizes the denigrating self-image passed on to women. He writes:

> Countless psychological studies have shown that woman is still perceived by both men and women as Adam's rib—despite all the efforts of feminists from Lucy Stone to Simone de Beauvoir. That is, she is defined not in terms of her self, but in terms of her relation to men: Adam's rib, Adam's temptress, Adam's helpmate, Adam's wife and mother of his children. The female image is characterized as small, weak, soft, and light. In the U.S., it is also dull, peaceful, relaxed, cold, rounded, passive and slow . . .
>
> Who wants to be small, weak, light, dull? Women must be pretty feeble creatures, pale reflections of men, by this definition. No wonder they have been dissatisfied with the image and have reacted with either open resentment or secret doubts as to their real worth.[3]

Girls and women are taught to be socially irrelevant, passive, to hide their natural abilities, to fear self-expression, lest they be called a "castrating" woman. When people are taught that they are inferior, and when society demands that they act inferior, it is not surprising that they appear to be inferior.

> There is an almost exact parallel between the role of women and the role of black people in this society. Together they constitute the great maintenance force sustaining the white American male. They wipe his

[2] Esther Peterson, "Working Women," *The Women in America,* Houghton Mifflin, 1965.

[3] David C. McClelland, "Wanted: A New Self-Image for Women," *The Woman in America,* Houghton Mifflin, 1965.

ass and breast-feed him when he is little, they school him in his youthful years, do his clerical work and raise his and their replacements later. All through his life in the factories, on the migrant farms, in the restaurants, hospitals, offices, and homes, they sew, stoop, cook, clean, sweep and run errands for him, haul away his garbage, and nurse him when his frail body falters.

BEVERLY JONES, *TOWARD A FEMALE LIBERATION MOVEMENT* (1968)

Women's liberation as a movement is young, radical and politically experienced. Its goals and actions are far more militant than the moderate and matronly National Organization for Women (founded by Betty Friedan). While women's liberation supports the struggle against occupational discrimination, its main thrust is against the institution of male chauvinism and the social and economic exploitation of all women. The reasons for this are not surprising.

The women's movement is a product of the experience of many hundreds of young women in the civil rights movement and in the urban white organizing undertaken by white, radical youth after the collapse of the civil rights movement. Young women and girls risked their lives in the struggle to create a just and humane society. They were beaten in demonstrations, they were arrested, and they were often sexually mistreated. They served time in jail, staffed the freedom houses, cranked the mimeograph machines, washed the dishes, loved the men, and cared for the children. Only to discover themselves absent from the steering committees, silent during meetings, and ridiculed when they protested that they had worked and risked their lives in organizations in which they had little power to make decisions. The young women learned that in a freedom struggle, they were not free.

Out of this contradiction, the women's liberation movement was born. At first, women asked only that they be permitted to participate in "participatory" democracy. This very reasonable and just request was laughed down by the young men, and so women learned at last just what male chauvinism must mean for their own movement:

One of the best things that ever happened to black militants happened when they got hounded out of the stars-and-stripes, white-controlled civil rights movement, when they started fighting for blacks instead of the American Dream. The best thing that ever happened to potential white radicals in civil rights happened when they got thrown out by SNCC and were forced to face their own oppression in their own world. When they started fighting for control of the universities, against the draft, the war, and the business order. And the best thing that may yet happen to potentially radical young women is that they will be driven out of both of these groups. That they will be forced to stop fighting for the "movement" and start fighting primarily for the liberation and independence of women. (Beverly Jones, *Toward a Female Liberation Movement*)

The young women's liberation movement (with groups in every major city in the United States and Canada) has learned from the struggle for equality for black people. It has learned to distrust legal "solutions" and to be militant. Its political analysis rests upon the assertion that "there is an almost exact parallel between the role of women and the role of black people." How do we evaluate this analysis? How close is the analogy? The work of three sociologists can help us to answer these questions.

The first is Gunnar Myrdal, author of *An American Dilemma,* a classic study of racism in the U.S. In the forgotten "appendix 5" of that work, the similarity of beliefs about black people and women was first drawn. A second sociologist, Everett C. Hughes, drew the same parallel in 1949. He points out that

People are accustomed to act toward women in certain ways. Likewise the Negro has a traditional role. The traditional roles of neither woman nor Negro include that of physician. Hence, when either of them becomes a physician the question arises whether to treat her or him as a physician or as woman or as Negro. Likewise, on their part, there is the problem whether, in a given troublesome situation, to act completely as physician or in the other role. This is their dilemma.[4]

It is clear that Hughes sees marginal blacks and marginal women as free-thinkers and as rebels, struggling against con-

[4] Everett C. Hughes, "Social Change and Status Protest: An Essay on the Marginal Man," *Phylon,* Vol. X.

servative conventions, and yet paying a heavy price for their struggle.

Helen Hacker, a sociologist, drawing upon Myrdal, has given us the most complete analysis of the parallels between white racism and male chauvinism. She points out that "the relationship between women and Negroes is historical as well as analogical. In the seventeenth century the legal status of Negro servants was borrowed from that of women and children, who were under the *patria potestas,* and until the Civil War there was considerable cooperation between the Abolitionist and the women suffrage movements." The following chart is taken from Helen Hacker's analysis of the situation in 1951.

Chart 1. Castelike Status of Women and Negroes[5]

Negroes	Women
1. High Social Visibility	
a. skin color, other "racial" characteristics	a. secondary sex characteristics
b. (sometimes) distinctive dress (and manners)*	b. distinctive dress (special codes of etiquette)*
2. Ascribed Attributes	
a. inferior intelligence, smaller brain, less convoluted, scarcity of genius	a. ditto
b. more free in instinctual gratification. More emotional, "primitive" and childlike. Imagined sexual prowess envied.	b. irresponsible, inconsistent, emotionally unstable, lack strong superego, women as temptresses (more intuitive, irrational)*
c. common stereotype "inferior"	c. "weaker" (women as incomplete men)*
3. Rationalization of Status	
a. thought all right in his place	a. woman's place is in the home
b. myth of contented Negro	b. myth of contented woman—"feminine" woman is happy in subordinate role

[5] Helen Hacker, "Women as a Minority Group," *Social Forces,* Vol. 30, p. 65.

4. Discrimination	
a. limitations on education, should fit "place" in society	a. ditto
b. confined to traditional jobs—barred from supervisory positions	b. ditto
c. deprived of political importance	c. ditto
d. social and professional segregation	d. ditto
e. more vulnerable to criticism	e. ditto

5. Accommodation Attitudes	
a. supplicatory whining intonation of voice	a. rising inflection, smiles, laughs, downward glances
b. deferential manner	b. flattering manner
c. concealment of real feelings	c. "feminine wiles"
d. outwit "white folks"	d. outwit "menfolk"
e. careful study of points at which dominant group is susceptible to influence	e. ditto
f. fake appeals for directives; show of ignorance	f. appearance of helplessness

Starred points in parentheses added by Dixon.

What Helen Hacker, as a sociologist, analyzed academically in 1951, the young women of the movement by 1966-68 had learned through direct and harsh experience. But they had also learned more:

Women who would avoid or extricate themselves from the common plight described, who would begin new lives, new movements, and new worlds, must first learn to acknowledge the reality of their present condition. They have got to reject the blind and faulty categories of thought foisted on them by a male order for its own benefit. . . . There is something horribly repugnant in the picture of women performing the same menial chores all day, having almost interchangeable conversations with their children, engaging in standard television arguments with their husbands, and then in the late hours of the night, each agonizing over what is considered her personal lot, her personal relationship, her personal problem. . . . Purposely divided from each other, each of us is ruled by one or more men for the benefit of all men. There is no personal escape, no personal salvation, no personal solution. (Beverly Jones, *Toward a Female Liberation Movement 1968)*

Institutionalized male chauvinism, like institutionalized white racism, is a social and political problem; it will only be solved through social and political change. American society has taught young women that the only way the oppressed people of this society gain their rights and their freedom is to fight for them. Women's liberation is committed to this struggle.

Helmer: Before all else you are a wife and mother.
Nora: That I no longer believe. I believe that
before all else I am a human being, just
as much as you are—or at least that I
should try to become one.
HENRIK IBSEN, *A DOLL'S HOUSE, 1879*

Women's liberation cries out for human freedom, for the right of every individual to create his or her own life and to develop fully his or her potential. To seek freedom forces us to oppose oppression of all people, black and white and female. The women's movement is based on a simple truth: we cannot set others free if we are not ourselves free. As women struggle against their fear of being inferior, as they seek ways of life that will truly permit them to be "before all else a human being," they increasingly discover themselves forced to take a militant stance, forced to accept the harsh truth that women's freedom will only be possible in a radically transformed society. Still the truth also means that each of us must become in important ways free women, unafraid and sure. So we may end as we began with a minor poet, who so movingly foresaw the spirit of the New Woman:

I will be no docile thing—
But a restless eagle in space
Threshing is better than sowing
I have spread the seeds too long!
Now there is a rich harvest of the unknown—
Riot and strange thoroughfares
There is din of thunder
And storm in the air
Like the rumble of guns from afar . . .
I cannot be this ordered self forever!
BLANCHE SHOEMAKER WAGSTAFF, *ATAVISM*

Metamorphosis into Bureaucrat
By Marge Piercy

My hips are a desk.
From my ears hang
chains of paperclips.
Rubber bands form my hair.
My breasts are wells of mimeograph ink.
My feet bear casters.
Buzz. Click.
My head
is a badly organized file.
My head is a switchboard
where crossed lines crackle.
My head is a wastebasket
of worn ideas.
Press my fingers
and in my eyes appear
credit and debit
zing. Tinkle.
My navel is a reject button.
From my mouth issue cancelled reams.
Swollen, heavy, rectangular
I am about to be delivered
of a baby
xerox machine.
File me under W
because I wonce
was
a woman.

♀ Double Jeopardy: To Be Black and Female

VENUS BETRAYED
Mark Bulwinkle

In attempting to analyze the situation of the black woman in America, one crashes abruptly into a solid wall of grave misconceptions, outright distortions of fact and defensive attitudes on the part of many. The system of capitalism (and its afterbirth—racism) under which we all live has attempted by many devious ways and means to destroy the humanity of all people, and particularly the humanity of black people. This has meant an outrageous assault on every black man, woman and child who resides in the United States.

In keeping with its goal of destroying the black race's will to

By Frances M. Beal 

resist its subjugation, capitalism found it necessary to create a situation where it was impossible for the black man to find meaningful or productive employment. More often than not, he couldn't find work of any kind. The black woman likewise was manipulated by the system, economically exploited and physically assaulted. She could often find work in the white man's kitchen, however, and sometimes became the sole breadwinner of the family. This predicament has led to many psychological problems on the part of both man and woman and has contributed to the turmoil found in the black family structure.

Unfortunately, neither the black man nor the black woman understood the true nature of the forces working upon them. Many black women accepted the capitalist evaluation of manhood and womanhood and believed, in fact, that black men were shiftless and lazy, that otherwise they would get a job and support their families as they ought to. Personal relationships between black men and women were torn asunder, and one result has been the separation of husband from wife, mother from child, etc.

America has defined the roles to which each individual should subscribe. It has defined "manhood" in terms of its own interests and "femininity" likewise. An individual who has a good job, makes a lot of money and drives a Cadillac is a real "man," and conversely, an individual who is lacking in these "qualities" is less of a man. The advertising media in this country continuously inform the American male of his need for indispensable signs of his virility—the brand of cigarettes that cowboys prefer, the whiskey that has a masculine tang or the label of the jock strap that athletes wear.

The ideal model that is projected for a woman is to be surrounded by hypocritical homage and estranged from all real work, spending idle hours primping and preening, obsessed with conspicuous consumption, and limited in function to simply a sex role. We unqualitatively reject these models. A woman who stays at home caring for children and the house often leads an extremely sterile existence. She must lead her entire life as a satellite to her mate. He goes out into society and brings back a little piece of the world for her. His interests and his understanding of the world become her own and she cannot develop herself as an individual, having been reduced to a biological function. This kind of woman leads a parasitic existence that can aptly be described as "legalized prostitution."

Futhermore, it is idle dreaming to think of black women simply caring for their homes and children like the middle-class white model. Most black women have to work to help house, feed and clothe their families. Black women make up a substantial percentage of the black working force from the pooorest black family to the so-called "middle-class" family.

Black women were never afforded such phony luxuries. Though we have been browbeaten with this white image, the reality of the degrading and dehumanizing jobs that were relegated to us quickly dissipated this mirage of womanhood. The following excerpt from a speech that Sojourner Truth made at a Women's Rights Convention in the 19th century shows us how misleading and incomplete a life this model represents for us:

> . . . Well, chilern, whar dar is so much racket dar must be something out o'kilter. I tink dat 'twixt de niggers of de Souf and de women at de Norf all a talkin' 'bout rights, de white men will be in a fix pretty soon. But what's all dis here talkin' 'bout? Dat man ober dar say dat women needs to be helped into carriages, and lifted ober ditches, and to have de best place every whar. Nobody ever help me into carriages, or ober mud puddles, or gives me any best places, . . . and ar'nt I a woman? Look at me! Look at my arm! . . . I have plowed, and planted, and gathered into barns, and no man could head me—and ar'nt I a woman? I could work as much as a man (when I could get it), and bear de lash as well—and ar'nt I a woman? I have borne five chilern and I seen 'em mos' all sold off into slavery, and when I cried out with a mother's grief, none but Jesus heard—and ar'nt I a woman?

Unfortunately, there seems to be some confusion in the Movement today as to who has been oppressing whom. Since the advent of black power, the black male has exerted a more prominent leadership role in our struggle for justice in this country. He sees the system for what it really is for the most part, but where he rejects its values and mores on many issues, when it comes to women, he seems to take his guidelines from the pages of the *Ladies' Home Journal*. Certain black men are maintaining that they have been castrated by society but that black women somehow escaped this persecution and even contributed to this emasculation.

The black woman in America can justly be described as a "slave of a slave." Since the black man in America was reduced to such abject oppression, the black woman had no protector and was used, and is still being used in some cases, as the scapegoat for the evils that this horrendous system has perpetrated on black men. Her physical image has been maliciously maligned; she has been sexually molested and abused by the white colonizer; she has suffered the worst kind of economic exploitation, having been forced to serve as the white woman's maid and as wet nurse for white offspring while her own children were, more often than not, starving and neglected. It is the depth of degradation to be socially manipulated, physically raped, used to undermine your own household, and to be powerless to reverse this situation.

It is true that our husbands, fathers, brothers and sons have been emasculated, lynched and brutalized. They have suffered from the cruelest assault on mankind that the world has ever known. However, it is a gross distortion of fact to state that black women have oppressed black men. The capitalist system found it expedient to enslave and oppress them and proceeded to do so without consultation or the signing of any agreements with black women.

It must also be pointed out at this time that black women are not resentful of the rise to power of black men. We welcome it. We see in it the eventual liberation of all black people from this corrupt system of capitalism. However, it is fallacious to think that in order for the black man to be strong, the black woman must be weak.

Those who are exerting their "manhood" by telling black women to step back into a domestic, submissive role are assuming a counterrevolutionary position. Black women, likewise, have been abused by the system, and we must begin talking about the elimination of all kinds of oppression. If we are talking about building a strong nation, capable of throwing off the yoke of capitalist oppression, then we are talking about the total involvement of every man, woman, and child, each with a highly developed political consciousness. We need our whole army out there dealing with the enemy, not half an army.

There are also some black women who feel that there is no more productive role in life than having and raising children. This attitude often reflects the conditioning of the society in which we live and is adopted from a bourgeois white model. Some young sisters who have never had to maintain a household or to accept the confinement which this entails, tend to romanticize (along with the help of a few brothers) the role of housewife and mother. Black women who have had to endure this function are less apt to have such utopian visions.

Those who portray in an intellectual manner how great and rewarding this role will be, and who feel that the most important thing that they can contribute to the black nation is children, are doing themselves a great injustice. This reasoning completely negates the contributions that black women such as Sojourner Truth, Harriet Tubman, Mary McLeod Bethune, and Fannie Lou Hamer have historically made to our struggle for liberation.

We live in a highly industrialized society, and every member of the black nation must be as academically and technologically developed as possible. To wage a revolution, we need competent teachers, doctors, nurses, electronics experts, chemists, biologists, physicists, political scientists, and so on. Black women sitting at home reading bedtime stories to their children are just not going to make it.

Economic Exploitation of Black Women

Capitalism finds it expedient to reduce women to a state of enslavement. They often serve as a scapegoat for the evils of this system. Much in the same way that the poor white cracker of the South, who is equally victimized, looks down upon blacks and contributes to the oppression of blacks, so, by giving to men a false feeling of superiority (at least in their own homes or in their relationships with women), the oppression of women acts as an escape valve for capitalism. Men may be cruelly exploited and subjected to all sorts of dehumanizing tactics on the part of the ruling class, but at least they're not women.

Women also represent a surplus labor supply, the control of which is absolutely necessary to the profitable functioning of capitalism. Women are systematically exploited by the system. They are paid less for the same work that men do, and jobs that are specifically relegated to women are low-paying and without the possibility of advancement. Statistics from the Women's Bureau of the U.S. Department of Labor show that in 1967, the wage scale for non-white women was the lowest of all:

White Males	$ 6,704
Non-White Males	$ 4,277
White Females	$ 3,991
Non-White Females	$ 2,861

Those industries which employ mainly black women are the most exploitative. Domestic and hospital workers are good examples of this oppression, as are the garment workers in New York City. The International Ladies Garment Workers Union (ILGWU) whose overwhelming membership consists of black and Puerto Rican women has a leadership that is nearly all lily white and male. This leadership has been working in collusion with the ruling class and has completely sold its soul to the corporate structure.

To add insult to injury, the ILGWU has invested heavily in business enterprises in racist, apartheid South Africa—with union funds. Not only does this bought-off leadership contribute to our continued exploitation in this country by not truly representing the best interests of its membership, but it audaciously uses funds that black and Puerto Rican women have provided to support the economy of a vicious government that is engaged in the economic rape and murder of our black brothers and sisters in our Motherland, Africa.

The entire labor movement in the United States has suffered as a result of the super-exploitation of black workers and women. The unions have historically been racist and chauvinist. They have upheld racism in this country and have failed to fight the white skin privileges of white workers. They have failed to fight or even make an issue against the inequities in the hiring and pay of women workers. There has been virtually no struggle against either the racism of the white worker or the economic exploitation of the working woman, two factors which have consistently impeded the advancement of the real struggle against the ruling class.

This racist, chauvinist and manipulative use of black workers and women, especially black women, has been a severe cancer on the American labor scene. It therefore becomes essential for those who understand the workings of capitalism and imperialism to realize that the exploitation of black people and women works to everyone's disadvantage and that the liberation of these two groups is a stepping stone to the liberation of all oppressed people in this country and around the world.

Bedroom Politics

I have briefly discussed the economic and psychological manipulation of black women, but perhaps the most outlandish act of oppression in modern times is the current campaign to promote sterilization of non-white women in an attempt to maintain the population and power imbalance between the white haves and the non-white have-nots.

These tactics are but another example of the many devious schemes that the ruling class elite attempts to perpetrate on the black population in order to keep itself in control. A massive campaign for so-called "birth control" is presently being promoted not only in the underdeveloped non-white areas of the world, but also in black communities here in the United States. However, what the authorities in charge of these programs refer to as "birth control" is in fact nothing but a method of surgical genocide.

The United States has been sponsoring sterilization clinics in non-white countries, especially in India, where already some 3 million young men and boys in and around New Delhi have been sterilized in makeshift operating rooms set up by American Peace Corps workers. Under these circumstances, it is understandable why certain countries view the Peace Corps not as a benevolent project, not as evidence of America's concern for underdeveloped areas, but rather as a threat to their very existence. This program could more aptly be named "The Death Corps."

The vasectomy, which is performed on males and takes only six or seven minutes, is a relatively simple operation. The sterilization of a woman, on the other hand, is admittedly major surgery. This operation (salpingectomy)* must be performed in a hospital under general anesthesia. This method of "birth control" is a common procedure in Puerto Rico. Puerto Rico has long been used by the colonialist exploiter, the United States, as an experimental laboratory for medical research before allowing certain practices to be imported and used here. When the birth control pill was first being perfected, it was tried out on Puerto Rican women and selected black women (poor), using them like guinea pigs to evaluate its effect and its efficiency.

The salpingectomy has now become the most common operation in Puerto Rico, more common than an appendectomy or a tonsillectomy. It is so widespread that it is referred to simply as "la operación." *On the Island, 20 percent of the women between the ages of 15 and 45 have already been sterilized.*

Now, as previously occurred with the pill, this method has been imported into the United States. Sterilization clinics are cropping up around the country in the black and Puerto Rican communities. These so-called "Maternity Clinics," specifically outfitted to purge black women and men of their reproductive possibilities, are appearing more and more in hospitals and clinics across the country.

A number of organizations have been formed to popularize the idea of sterilization, such as The Association for Voluntary Sterilization and The Human Betterment (!!!?) Association for Voluntary Sterilization, Inc., which has its headquarters in New

* Salpingectomy: through an abdominal incision, the surgeon cuts both Fallopian tubes and ties off the separated ends, so that there is no way for the egg to pass from the ovary to the womb.

York City. Front Royal, Virginia, has one such "Maternity Clinic" in Warren Memorial Hospital. The tactics used in the clinic in Fauquier County, Virginia, where poor and helpless black mothers and young girls are pressured into undergoing sterilization are certainly not confined to that clinic alone.

Threatened with the cut-off of relief funds, some black welfare women have been forced to accept this sterilization procedure in exchange for a continuation of welfare benefits. Mt. Sinai Hospital in New York City performs these operations on many of its ward patients whenever it can convince the women to undergo this surgery. Mississippi and some of the other Southern states are notorious for this act. Black women are often afraid to permit any kind of necessary surgery because they know from bitter experience that they are more likely than not to come out of the hospital without their insides. Both salpingectomies and hysterectomies are performed.

We condemn this use of the black woman as a medical testing ground for the white middle class. Reports of ill effects, including deaths, from the use of the birth control pill only started to come to light when the white privileged class began to be affected. These outrageous Nazi-like procedures on the part of medical researchers are but another manifestation of the totally amoral and dehumanizing brutality that the capitalist system perpetrates on black women. The sterilization experiments carried on in concentration camps some twenty-five years ago have been denounced the world over, but no one seems to get upset by the repetition of these same racist tactics today in the United States of America—land of the free and home of the brave. This campaign is as nefarious a program as Germany's gas chambers and, in a long term sense, as effective and with the same objective.

The rigid laws concerning abortions in this country are another vicious means of subjugation and, indirectly, of outright murder. Rich white women somehow manage to obtain these operations with little or no difficulty. It is the poor black and Puerto Rican woman who is at the mercy of the local butcher. Statistics show that the non-white death rate at the hands of unqualified abortionists is substantially higher than for white women. Nearly half of the child-bearing deaths in New York City are attributed to abortion alone, and out of these, 79 percent are among non-white and Puerto Rican women.

We are not saying that black women should not practice birth control. Black women have the right and the responsibility to determine when it is *in the interest of the struggle to have children or not to have them and this right must not be relinquished to anyone*. It is also the black woman's right and responsibility to determine when it is in her own best interest to have children, how many she will have, and how far apart. Forced sterilization practices, abortion laws, and the unavailability of safe birth control methods are all symptoms of a decadent society that jeopardizes the health of black women (and thereby the entire black race) in its attempts to control the very life processes of human beings. These are symptoms of a society that believes it has the right to bring political factors into the privacy of the bedchamber. The elimination of these horrendous conditions will free black women for full participation in the revolution and, thereafter, in the building of the new society.

Relationship to White Movement

Much has been written recently about the white women's liberation movement in the United States, and the question arises whether there are any parallels between this struggle and the movement on the part of black women for total emancipation. While there are certain comparisons that one can make, simply because we both live under the same exploitative system, there are certain differences, some of which are quite basic.

The white women's movement is far from being monolithic. Any white group that does not have an anti-imperialist and anti-racist ideology has nothing in common with the black woman's struggle. In fact, some groups come to the incorrect conclusion that their oppression is due simply to male chauvinism. They therefore have an extremely anti-male tone. Black people are engaged in a life and death struggle and the main emphasis of black women must be to combat the capitalist, racist exploitation of black people. While it is true that male chauvinism has become institutionalized in American society, one must always look for the main enemy—the fundamental cause of the condition of females.

Another major differentiation is that the white women's liberation movement is basically middle class. Very few of these women suffer the extreme economic exploitation that most black women are subjected to day by day. This is the factor that is most crucial for us. It is not an intellectual persecution alone, it is not an intellectual outburst for us; it is quite real. We as black women have got to deal with the problems that the black masses deal with, for our problems in reality are one and the same.

If the white groups do not realize that they are in fact fighting capitalism and racism, we do not have common bonds. If they do not realize that the reasons for their condition lie in the system and not simply that men get a vicarious pleasure out of "consuming their bodies for exploitative reasons" (this reasoning seems to be quite prevalent in certain white women's groups), then we cannot unite with them around common grievances or even discuss these groups in a serious manner because they're completely irrelevant to the black struggle.

The New World

The black community and black women especially must begin raising questions about the kind of society we wish to see established. We must note the ways in which capitalism oppresses us and then move to create institutions that will eliminate these destructive influences.

The new world that we are attempting to create must destroy oppression of every type. The value of this new system will be determined by the status of the person who was lowest on the totem pole. Unless women in any enslaved nation are completely liberated, the change cannot really be called a revolution. If the black woman has to retreat to the position she occupied before the armed struggle, the whole movement and the whole struggle will have retreated in terms of truly freeing the colonized population.

A people's revolution that engages the participation of every member of the community, including man, woman, and child, brings about a certain transformation in the participants as a result of this participation. Once we have caught a glimpse of freedom or experienced a bit of self-determination, we can't go back to old routines that were established under a racist, capitalist regime. We must begin to understand that a revolution entails not only the willingness to lay our lives on the firing line and get killed. In some ways, this is an easy commitment to make. To die for the revolution is a one-shot deal; to live for the revolution means taking on the more difficult commitment of changing our day-to-day life patterns.

This will mean changing the traditional routines that we have established as a result of living in a totally corrupting society. It means changing how one relates to one's wife, husband, parents and co-workers. If we are going to liberate ourselves as a people, it must be recognized that black women have very specific problems that have to be spoken to. We must be liberated along with the rest of the population. We cannot wait to start working on those problems until that great day in the future when the revolution somehow, miraculously, is accomplished.

To assign women the role of housekeeper and mother while men go forth into battle is a highly questionable doctrine for a revolutionary to maintain. Each individual must develop a high political consciousness in order to understand how this system enslaves us all and what actions we must take to bring about its total destruction. Those who consider themselves to be revolutionary must begin to deal with other revolutionaries as equals. So far as I know, revolutionaries are not determined by sex.

Old people, young people, men and women must take part in the struggle. To relegate women to purely supportive roles or to purely cultural considerations is dangerous. Unless black men who are preparing themselves for armed struggle understand that the society which we are trying to create is one in which the oppression of *all members* of that society is eliminated, then the revolution will have failed in its avowed purpose.

Given the mutual commitment of black men and black women alike to the liberation of our people and other oppressed peoples around the world, the total involvement of each individual is necessary. A revolutionary has the responsibility not only to topple those who are now in a position of power, but to create new institutions that will eliminate all forms of oppression. We must begin to rewrite our understanding of traditional personal relationships between man and woman. All the resources that the black community can muster must be channeled into the struggle. Black women must take an active part in bringing about the kind of society where our children, our loved ones, and each citizen can grow up and live as decent human beings, free from the pressures of racism and capitalist exploitation.

Birthright
By Margo Magid

This
is a woman:
to be born half
hollow, to weave
empty baskets
that words sink through,
and to wait
somewhere
beyond hands
in rooms she builds
to fill with midnight
tears, and wait
a thousand journals
for a crippled poem
that never shows,
and wait
with heavy arms
for the seed
he will not give.
Women are worse
than vessels,
holding broken
stems that only
children heal

♀ As a student at one of our nation's most liberal and (I think) advanced universities, I have long been outraged by the way women are treated, by men and by women. The Double Standard runs rampant, abortions are relegated to dirty back rooms, and women's salaries lag behind men's. Moreover, people justify all this by naming as God's Law what is really only man's.

I am sure you will receive a great deal of criticism on this issue. But I have found that no matter how justified or humane I may be, whenever I say what people are not used to hearing I can expect to be criticized. The fact that people oppose you means only that they cannot ignore what you are saying.

There is nothing unfeminine about me, either in appearance or in instincts. But I fail to see anything funny —or "cute"—about my wanting to get a Ph.D., and not at night after changing diapers all day. If people feel threatened by my asserting myself as an individual and as an intellectual, then maybe they had better ask themselves why.

Waltham, Massachusetts

♀ In regard to your *motive* issue of March and April, I disagree with your attitude. I am 20 years old and I dearly love my womanhood. I am entering my senior year at Franklin College this fall. I have, at present, a 3.02 accumulative average. I am a member of the Theatrical Honorary. I am majoring in Theatre Arts–Acting. I consider myself an intelligent and logically minded woman.

I love my femininity and womanliness and I am proud of my sex. I like to have men open doors for me, hold my chair, help me with my coat.

Sure, I am frustrated at times when my opinion is not valued as highly as those of the men around me just because I am a woman. This doesn't happen very often, though. I find that any woman who has a valid opinion about pertinent issues will find acceptance if her opinions are, in fact, valid.

My point in writing this letter is that I wish you all to look into the future and see what will happen if you achieve your goals in liberating the women of this country. Our children will no longer look to us as their ever-loving mothers but rather another bread-winner. Our husbands will no longer look at us adoringly as feminine, lovely, loving women but rather a fellow-worker.

I look forward to the day when I can put a Mrs. in front of my name; to the day when a small child will look at me adoringly and say, "Mommy, I love you."

Please, in your quest, remember those of us who love our womanhood. Don't ruin it for us. If you don't want to get married and have children, don't. If you feel it is a burden to be a wife and a mother, then you haven't the right to be either. But don't speak for all of us in your campaign because some of us cherish the love we will give and receive with our future families.

Glenside, Pennsylvania

♀ The very *fact* of the woman issue of *motive* has long distance phone calls going and coming across the country among lots of different networks of women I know; some were in touch with the movement before, some weren't. So here's some good feedback to you via the image of women running to the telephone: they're too excited to sit down and write letters to each other.

The issue itself—image and format-wise—is great. Especially the frontispiece. Haven't finished reading all the articles yet, but so far, they're all right on target. Especially Ozick's.

Chicago, Illinois

♀ I, as you, have the youthful illusion that I can succeed in "making something of myself," and it was quite pleasant to find someone has retained the faith. However—

What is this complete equality you speak of? Who among those of you "WOMEN writers" would shoulder your guns on the front line of Viet Nam? Surely we cannot expect the harvest of equality without the chaff?

Fair or unfair, *that* is equality.

Saint Joseph, Missouri

THE BRIDE AND HER MATRON OF HONOR
Judith Stevens Sayfie

♀

The Subversion of Betty Crocker

Next time you pass a newsstand or magazine counter, notice what's on sale. Here in New York, typically, you'll find about three dozen magazines, nearly two dozen of which will be women's magazines. Why? Because they sell. Notice also the variety: general-interest magazines aimed mostly (although not exclusively) at housewives—*Ladies' Home Journal, McCall's, Good Housekeeping, Redbook;* general-interest magazines aimed mostly at unmarried women—*Seventeen* and *Ingénue* for younger women, *Cosmopolitan* and *Single Girl* for older ones; special-subject magazines—*Modern Bride* and others aimed at about-to-be-married women, magazines about hair styles and care, cosmetics, knitting, sewing; fashion/beauty magazines—*Glamour* and *Mademoiselle, Vogue* and *Harper's Bazaar;* plus *True Confessions, Modern Romance, Screenlife, Silver Screen* and countless other romance magazines and comic books.

Each of these magazines is aimed at a slightly different audience and thus emphasizes different aspects of the image of American women (their readers). *Seventeen* and *Ingénue* for the teenage-into-early college age bracket; *Glamour* and *Mademoiselle* for the college/young-working-girl/young mother group; *Vogue* and *Harper's Bazaar* for the very rich and for those of us who like to peek at the way the rich live. Then there's a bundle directed at married women (predominantly)—*Ladies' Home Journal, McCall's, Family Circle, Good Housekeeping, Better Homes & Gardens, Woman's Day, House Beautiful, Redbook*—each of which has (or tries to have) a special emphasis. *Better Homes & Gardens* carries gardening features that the others don't (or don't regularly). *Good Housekeeping* and *Family Circle* emphasize food, often budget food. *Woman's Day* goes in for do-it-yourself projects. *McCall's* and the *Ladies' Home Journal* are "more sophisticated" in fashions, food, beauty features: which means they're aimed at a more up-

By Susan Sutheim ♀

wardly mobile, urban-suburban audience than, e.g., *Redbook*.

Any woman could probably produce the same rundown of women's magazines, and supply all sorts of details and point out distinctions I've skipped. This may be partially because most women buy one or more women's magazines from time to time. This familiarity also stems from the fact—and this is important—that we read our mothers' magazines from the time we're seven or eight. I can recall, at age nine, telling my mother about an article I'd just read in the *Ladies' Home Journal* about how Russians are just ordinary nice people. This, in 1951, produced a rather hysterical reaction from my mother, who threatened to cancel her subscription. Subversive literature right in her own living room!

Which was precisely the point; if the mothers are resistant, you can indoctrinate the kids. (Skeptics who think girls don't read their mothers' magazines should take a look at the February 1969 *McCall's,* in which the beginning of a new feature by and for under-14-year-olds is announced.)

I said magazines indoctrinate their readers. That's a strong word, and it demands explanation. Just who is indoctrinating whom, and to what end?

I worked for a year in the food department for the *Ladies' Home Journal*. During that year I learned how editorial decisions are generally made, about who has the power to veto editorial material, about how it gets in in the first place. I gather, from friends who work for other magazines and from reading advertising trade journals, that my experience was typical of the trade.

In magazines, you're dealing with two sets of people in business to make a profit: the publishers and hundreds of advertisers. The publisher earns his money by selling the magazine (subscriptions, newsstand sales), but more importantly, from the sale of advertising space in the pages of his magazine. (No magazine could sustain itself on subscriptions alone without raising subscription prices out of sight—and out of competitive range. So either you have foundation support or some other form of donated money, or you sell lots of ads.) Thus, from the publisher's and advertisers' points of view, a magazine exists to sell (run) ads; and the advertisers' desires (which are anyhow pretty much the same as the publisher's) generally determine editorial content.

Advertising space is access to a consumer market—the people who read the magazine. Hence elaborate, constant and expensive reader surveys: advertisers want to know where your readers live, what their educational level is, what occupations they (and/or their husbands) are in, how many children are in the average reader's family, what the average reader's income is, etc.

All this because in order to sell whatever it is you have to sell, you have to know whom you're talking to. The advertising copy—and to some extent, the product—you offer to a non-college-educated, $8,000-per-year suburban woman is not the same as that you address to a college-educated working mother in a large city, or to a single woman.

Given the fact that, from the viewpoint of publisher and advertiser, the ultimate goal of a women's magazine is to *sell* (the magazine, the products it advertises), what—in their estimation and experience—makes women buy? A quick survey of ads and the editorial copy that supplements them yields some obvious answers.

To wit: how does a wife and mother demonstrate her concern/love/devotion to her family? She bakes them a Betty Crocker/Pillsbury/Swans Down just-like-homemade cake. How does a woman secure her husband's wandering attention? She acts "like an expensive mistress" (demands a mink coat), as a recent *New York Times* ad put it. How does a woman explore and express her individuality? She tries an "exotic" or "offbeat" or "romantic" new lipstick, perfume, paint for the kitchen; she takes an exciting trip to Paris; she buys a cookbook and tries out an exotic recipe. In short, how does a woman (or any proper American) express who she is and how she relates to other people? She buys, buys, buys.

And if you don't have life insurance (get your husband to buy it), you're neglecting the future interests of your children. If you don't have a set of "good" china as well as dishes for everyday use, you're a bit plain, a bit common, a bit of a drag.

If you don't treat yourself to a new dress/hairdo/make-up once in a while, well, that's your business, but you really are needlessly denying yourself.

All of which is not to say that one ought not to enjoy a new dress, a trip to Paris, a new paint job for the kitchen, or whatever. All of which *is* to say that if you think such things—*things*—are sufficient satisfaction of basic human needs, sufficient expression of human relationships, you're in trouble. And given the overriding social pressure we live under, when in some corner of your mind you realize that something's missing, your urge will be to fill the gap with still another thing. Including such *things* as psychiatric therapy, going to a good movie, taking a course at a museum—in all cases one pays the price and gets what's paid for. (Even on the emotional level we deal in terms of prices exacted and paid. Consider the human meaning of familiar turns of phrase like "What is that relationship costing you emotionally? . . . I just can't afford an involvement, or commitment, of that sort.")

One of the main props of this commodity culture is the current—and classic—image of the American woman. She is feminine: nonaggressive, noncompetitive (with men), intuitive and instinctual (more than rational). She is physically beautiful (or at least committed to trying to be). She is loving, warm, sympathetic, mothering; as distinguished from (often opposed to) men, who are hard-headed, cold-blooded, selfish and authoritarian. Since the World War II era, when women were needed in large numbers to work in jobs left vacant by men going into the Army, it has become generally acceptable, even desirable, for women to work.

Over the last twenty years, the image of American women one commonly finds in women's magazines has changed. It has also remained basically unchanged. If you were to skim through all the back issues of a woman's magazine for the last twenty years (as I often did when I worked at the *Ladies' Home Journal*), you'd find the changes rather striking. Shortly after the end of World War II, when the men came home and women were no longer needed in the labor market in large numbers, there was a flood of articles, the general theme of which was:

"I used to work from nine to five and it was good because it was patriotic, but now I have returned to being 'just' a housewife again and it's great." This was supplemented by articles on the joys of motherhood, and how there's no such thing as "just" a housewife (a wife is a psychiatrist, a chauffeur, a mediator of disputes, a gourmet cook, a hobby expert, a laundress, seamstress, Girl Scout leader, civic helper, etc.).

By the late 1950's, this theme was not so frequent. And as the 1960's advanced, there began to appear another—and apparently quite contradictory—theme. Articles popped up which discussed whether one could manage to work and be a proper mother at the same time. Strictly family-oriented magazines introduced regular features aimed at the young, unmarried working girl. Feature articles about how it's possible (and desirable) to get away from the kids for a day or a week cropped up, along with articles about going back to school (often to get teaching credentials) at age forty ("My Daughter and I Are Classmates").

Supplementing this came ads whose general message was: explore your creative potential; don't (just) sit by the hearth; be a little wild, be a little extravagant; indulge yourself. Lipsticks were given exotic names—Pago Pago Peach, Mad Mocha. Perfumes hinted at indiscretion and just-this-side-of-illicit romance—Sirocco, Intimate, Indiscrète.

The new image of an adventurous, assertive, non-homebound woman seemed at odds with the stereotype of the passive, mothering, feminine woman. What happened to all those myths about how a Career Woman loses her femininity and becomes cold and competitive? If a woman makes a good consumer precisely because she's passive, relying on buying things to establish her identity and to express her purpose and relationships, wasn't this new image rather subversive—at least potentially?

Dead wrong. Point number one: all the adventurousness and it's-OK-to-have-a-career propaganda was, and is, firmly placed in an unchanged context: it's OK (good, even) to pursue a career—before you're married (or have kids), after your kids are grown, and/or while you're raising kids (if you can manage it, and plenty of women do). It's fine to be adventurous, go back to school, take a trip—but of course that doesn't mean *sacrificing* your role as wife and/or mother.

Point number two: an active, curious, well-educated, assertive woman is a much *better* consumer than a plain old passive woman. Not that there's anything wrong with passivity—it's just a bit old-fashioned, not very with-it, a bit hickish. An active woman develops all sorts of new tastes, new interests, new ways of fulfilling basic needs—and that means you can sell her all sorts of new products. Plain Jane might be so content with her domestic routine and so devoted to her family that she'd never buy a set of golf clubs, never indulge herself with a special beauty treatment, never slip away for a week alone in the sun. (Furthermore, Plain Jane is not likely to enjoy a family income great enough to do that sort of thing.) Bubbling Betty, on the other hand, finds time to golf on weekends, took a trip to Paris last year and flipped on French cooking (cookbooks, special cooking utensils, special food products), and has been thinking of spending a day in the city treating herself to a once-over facial and hairstyling. Bubbling Betty's husband probably earns upwards of $15,000 a year, and Betty herself may work part-time.

Confirmation that who and what women are supposed to be is comparable to what our grandmothers were supposed to be (with added fillips) comes in the February 1969 issue of several women's magazines. *McCall's, Glamour* and *Single Girl* include articles about "the sexual revolution" and its attendant problems. What they mean by "sexual revolution" is that many young people today are "cohabiting in an unmarried state." All the articles take it for granted that this is not a revolution in practice, but in frankness: our parents may have slept together, even lived together, before they were married; but they didn't do it openly.

OK, it's not that much of a revolution. But something is going on that women's magazines which never had touched this heretofore awkward subject have to deal with. On one level, women with teenage daughters have to figure out what to tell them about living with a man. Is it OK? Not OK? Sometimes OK? What are the limits of acceptability? From another angle, young women living with a man have to decide on what basis the relationship exists. Do they, should they, intend to get married? How soon? Why?

The parameters of acceptability are these: *Of course* marriage is the eventual goal of a living arrangement. *Single Girl* features an article on "How to Get the Man You're Living with to Marry You." The *McCall's* article thinks living arrangements are acceptable "because . . . they [young women] will be released from the pressures of early marriage, hasty marriage. . . ." The *Glamour* article details the agonies of several young women trying to figure out how to broach the subject, trying to decide whether to stick it out until the man in question is ready.

Parameter of acceptability number two: *of course* (OF COURSE) if you want to have children, you get married. In this case, much more is conveyed by what isn't said than by what is. None of the articles even remotely considers that a man and a woman might have a child and stay together, but not marry. A woman might raise a child by herself if, for whatever reason, she and the father split up; that's tough but not unheard of. What is entirely and literally unheard of is nonmarriage *and* sticking together *and* raising a family.

The point: the much-publicized sexual revolution is—or at least women's magazines say it is—no revolution at all when you consider what, under all the trimmings, the woman's role is. Even less of a revolution when you look at it in terms of social organization and not only in terms of a single person or family unit: the nuclear family remains the institution within which child-bearing and child-rearing take place; the nuclear family remains the single most important institution for the purchase of consumer goods. Tamper seriously with the nuclear family, and you're threatening the entire economy, the entire society.

Evidence: the article in *Glamour* notes that there are no statistics available on how many people are living together unmarried. Why? Because according to the Census Bureau, "cohabiting couples are not 'an important consumer entity.'" Consumer entity. Marriage, as they say on Madison Avenue (they really do say this) makes business; living arrangements don't. Sure, if you're living with someone you have to have dishes, food, blankets, clothes, plenty of things. But you're not going to buy life insurance, expensive rugs, "good" china or silver, or any of hundreds of major durable consumer goods (washing machine, vacuum cleaner, etc.). Which is to say, living arrangements that don't transform into marriage could be a sticky wicket for the people who sell life insurance, washing machines and so on.

More evidence about potential problems with living arrangements: the *McCall's* article has buried in it a dead-giveaway sentence. From the businessman's point of view the logic is backwards; it nevertheless is sound: "I need to find fixed and immutable aspects to the relationship of man and woman, and so I find them. I find them by refusing to accept a viable alternative to a stable family for the rearing of offspring."

Viable alternative for the rearing of offspring? Viable alternative to the nuclear family, the single most important motor of our consumption-crazy economy? If you're selling washing machines, that's not funny. It is very threatening. Moreover, it's not a vague off-in-the-future threat; it is happening.

It has begun to happen in and around the New Left, that multi-organizational, cultural/political monster that has already caused at least minor problems for American capitalism (take a look at *Fortune* magazine for January 1969 for an idea of how serious, potentially, the problems are). It's not yet a fully conscious or fully political phenomenon. People just live together. Why marry? It's a hassle—forms, licenses, bureaucracy, all of it meaningless. And it's much more of a hassle to get unmarried. So far, every New Left couple I know of who has a child is married (I think, and/or they say). Some people are speculating about what would happen if you had a child and didn't marry. No one really knows—yet. Much talk, also, about setting up day-care centers, about how to deal with raising our kids (not this couple's kids or that couple's; *our* kids). Plus, with very little talk (except some unfortunate pompousness that seems now to have ended), a lovely freedom from "things" has happened. Not that people don't enjoy a new record, not that we give up things and turn ascetic; we've broken the *compulsiveness* of consumption.

And with this, another political event has begun to connect hundreds of groups all over the country. There's no single, no central organization, but it is collectively known as the women's liberation movement. This movement has diverse sources; women who have been active in various New Left groups are into women's liberation, and so are women who never before in their lives have been politically aware or involved. One common element amidst the considerable diversity is an understanding/conviction/feeling that the image of womanhood we've been brought up with (the image that women's magazines convey) is wrong, bad, destructive. The fundamental wrongness is that we're supposed to believe we can satisfy our real needs by buying things and by buying things only. And of course we can't—which is precisely the point. Unsatisfied, we buy more, more, and more. Always a little hungry. Always seeing fulfillment just a little out of reach.

The political potential, the human potential, of this movement is enormous. We are half of humankind; we are 53% of America. We've been pinched and repressed and distorted in a thousand ways for a thousand years and more. Tap that sublimated and misdirected energy, and something's going to happen. Is happening. Soon it will become stylish; the *New York Times* printed in February a long—and quite sympathetic—article about the "women of the American revolution, 1969." Stylishness will not kill it, any more than the media really killed what was strong and liberating in the early hippie movement.

And the women's magazines? How will they accommodate this upheaval? Soon we will start seeing articles about furniture fashions for the liberated woman living with the liberated (swinging, chic, young) man. Soon will come articles about honeymoon-like vacations for the unmarried set. Soon will come articles detailing the horrors of being 35 and having lived with a man (or men) contentedly for years, and suddenly realizing you're all alone. And not quite so soon, but certainly on the agenda, are articles about the entirely disastrous consequences of trying to raise a child with a man you're not married to.

The consequences—plenty of them—will be disastrous, precisely to the degree to which people are left to deal with them alone. Enter once more the women's liberation movement and the New Left (of which it is a part), which bears promise of not having to deal with the consequences alone. If cohabitation without marriage and child-rearing without marriage (without relying on the nuclear family) are dealt with socially and politically—along with a vast number of other things, to be sure—we stand a chance of beginning to transform our society profoundly, and in immensely healthy ways.

Think of it just in terms of the development of a healthy, curious, confident, loving child. A hundred years ago, a child grew up in an extended family (parents, lots of brothers and sisters, grandparents, aunts, uncles, and their families). Grew up, in other words, used to being around a variety of people and not dependent only upon his parents for love, for identity-formation, for early learning. Contrast that with a child (I know too many) who grows up, until age three or four maybe, knowing the adult world only through his parents, with his parents as his only stable/frequent/reliable reference points. It's bad. It means (comparatively) limited ability to accept and relate to people who aren't your parents; it means your early (and partially definitive) interests, prejudices and skills are limited by those of your parents; it means, in short, going through critical formative years in a semi-deprived environment.

The women's liberation movement is real. It's growing so quickly that a standard complaint of every women's group I know of is that they don't know how to absorb new members fast enough. And one of the top items on our agenda is a redefinition of who we are. Step one in that redefinition is that we aren't who the women's magazines say we are, or ought to be. And redefining ourselves and how we live—*we're* doing the defining this time, not the guys who sell shampoo and refrigerators (and make a little napalm on the side). Redefining ourselves is what liberation is about.

The Playground (A Prose Poem)
By Leah Fritz

The iron gate is high and there are points. But this is a public garden and therefore treeless. The women sit and sweat over their children in the summertime. The children run under the spray in bathing suits when the spray is on, but this summer there is a draught.

Hamlet is a play about remembrance, remembrance and death. "Pray love, remember." "Rosemary is for remembrance." "Remember me."

Woman, that strange creature, strives—to be, uniquely to be. To be. What to be? How uniquely she understands the plight, victim that she is, of the great swindle. Did you say it wasn't cut off? Oh, but it was! You remind me of it every day. Caught. In a cage. The bars of iron have tidy points to rip the little chins that climb. Alarmed. At the swellings. And the braces. At the cough. At the growing up. Alarmed. To make of every day a happy day, of every minute happiness. We gossip in the park. Castrated. We watch the children play. Castrate them. This is mine to pass on to you. Remembrance. Pray, love. Remembrance of the dead, that you may die.

And did he scream at me? And did he say you don't know what you're talking about once too often? And did I kill him? Was it time for him to die? Did he say the same old thing? Did I grow tired of he said, she said, I said? And I discovered, it took a whole generation for me to discover, that I am right. So what do I tell you? Believe them, be safe. For another generation. I don't know what that means. Is it better safe? Is safe happy? Remember. The dead want you to remember. They have long memories. They come out of the sandbox and haunt you.

Play with the ball. Leave me alone. I'm talking to the ladies. It is hot. You are hot too? Listen, I've never lied to you. I never will. Make of your life. It's not much I gave you. I found that out too late. Make a sandpile. Make a pie. Eat, mein kind.

These are the ladies that push you. Into the playground and out. They don't know what they are talking about. No they don't. In their suits and their slacks and their empty voices, you hear me talk to

them to pass the time. You know it's foolish. Mama, come and play with me! I would be better off, but my depression, my morbid curiosity, sticks me to the bench. What will she say, this one, that I have heard before? Mommy, they just talk. I hate that talk.

So I swear a vow of silence. Mute I stand in my black robes against the wall of iron spikes that the children chin on I have heard that talk before I will not listen to another word but buy the groceries and check out at the check-out counter pick up my stamps and go. Before I go, give me one kiss. Oh, you are so sweet. Pray, love. Pray love, remember.

For a Brilliant Young Woman Who Lost Her Mind
By Rita Mae Brown

Sometimes I look at you
And wonder
How was it you
Were pulled under
And not myself?
Trapped in an undertow of pea-green rooms
Fourteen months you were coming up
From the sea
Of the mind drowned;
Coming to the beach
Where I
The first amphibian
Was moving unused legs.

WOODCUT: PREOCCUPATION
Lois Kojola

♀

The Realities of Lesbianism

The Lesbian minority in America, which may run as high as ten million women, is probably the least understood of all minorities and the most downtrodden. The Lesbian has two strikes on her from the start; she is a woman and she is a homosexual, a minority scorned by the vast majority of people in our country. If, in addition, she is a member of a racial minority, it is hard sometimes to understand how she survives.

A Lesbian is a woman who prefers another woman as a sexual partner; a woman who is drawn erotically to women rather than to men. This definition includes women who have never experienced overt sexual relations with a woman—the key word is "prefers." There is really no other valid way to define the Lesbian, for outside of the sexual area she is as different in her actions, dress, status and behavior as anyone else. Just as there is no typical heterosexual woman, neither is there any typical Lesbian.

However, there is a popular misconception, or stereotype, of the Lesbian. She is believed to embody all the worst masculine attributes of toughness, aggressiveness, lack of emotion, lack of sentiment, overemphasis on sex, lack of stability—the need and desire to dress as a man or, at least, as much like a man as possible.

At some time in her life the Lesbian may fit this stereotype—usually when she is very young and just finding out about herself. After all, the Lesbian is a product of her heterosexual environment, and all she has to go on, at her first awareness of Lesbian feeling in herself, is society's image. Part of the reason for her over-masculinization is the sexual identity of being attracted to women. At this point the Lesbian feels that in order to be attractive to another woman she must appear masculine. Another reason is for identification purposes. How will she meet other Lesbians? How will they know her to be one of them unless she indicates herself in her outward appearance?

By Del Martin and Phyllis Lyon

A third reason is one of releasing her hostility against society, of defying the mores which she finds stifling to what she considers her very being. A fourth reason is comfort. Any woman who says that girdles and high heels are comfortable is simply lying.

While it is true that occasionally a Lesbian gets trapped in this way of life (emulation of the male) and never finds her way to being a person rather than a symbol, the vast majority pass through this phase and learn to accept their femininity. As a Lesbian she comes to realize she is a human being first, a woman second, and a Lesbian only third. Unfortunately, however, society places the emphasis on the third—sexual identification—and does not acknowledge the Lesbian as a woman or a person.

But the average Lesbian (if there can be anything approaching "average" in our very complex world) is indistinguishable from other women in dress, in manner, in goals and desires, in actions and in interests. The difference lies only in that she looks to women for her emotional and sexual fulfillment. She is a member of the family—a distant cousin, or perhaps a maiden aunt. But more than likely she's closer to home—maybe a daughter, a wife and mother, a grandmother or a sister. She may work in an office, in a factory production line, in the public school system, at the corner grocery. She is not bound by lines of class distinction or educational level, race or religion.

What causes a woman to become a Lesbian? How can it be that two sisters, raised by the same parents in the same home, can turn in two different directions—one toward heterosexuality, the other toward homosexuality? Very simply, the answer is that no one knows. A great deal of research and study has been done in this country on the male homosexual, but very little has been done on the Lesbian. The reason for this, we suspect, lies in the status of women in our country. Because the male—masculinity—is so highly valued, it has been deemed to be imperative to search out the reasons for any deviation from this American norm. Also, the majority of persons working in research are men. Research on the Lesbian has, for the most part, been confined to women who were either psychiatric patients or in prison—which hasn't made for a very full or accurate picture.

Nevertheless, if you begin reading about the "causes" of homosexuality you will find that, as in the Bible, the answer you want to find will be somewhere. Each "expert" on the subject presents a different "cause." Our feeling, which is supported by a growing number of professional persons, is that homosexuality (in both men and women) is merely one dimension of the vastly complicated and varied spectrum of human sexuality. There has always been homosexuality; it has appeared in almost every culture in recorded history; it occurs in every species of animal.

Perhaps the most logical and least hysterical of all statements about homosexuality is the following made by Dr. Joel Fort, psychiatrist and public health specialist; Dr. Evelyn G. Hooker, research psychologist at the University of California at Los Angeles; and Dr. Joe K. Adams, psychologist and former mental health officer in California. The statement, made in August of 1966, is as follows:

> Homosexuals, like heterosexuals, should be treated as individual human beings, not as a special group, either by law or social agencies or employers.
>
> Laws governing sexual behavior should be reformed to deal only with clearly antisocial behavior, such as behavior involving violence or youth. The sexual behavior of individual adults by mutual consent in private should not be a matter of public concern.
>
> Some homosexuals, like some heterosexuals, are ill; some homosexuals, like some heterosexuals, are preoccupied with sex as a way of life. But probably for a majority of adults their sexual orientation constitutes only one component of a much more complicated life style.

Why then, if the Lesbian is by and large indistinguishable from other women and if her sexuality is not abnormal, does she face such genuine problems in her search for self-fulfillment? For struggle she does against myriad obstacles presented to her by a hostile society. Through our work with the Daughters of Bilitis, Inc., a Lesbian organization started in San Francisco in 1955, we have talked to literally thousands of Lesbians (and almost as many male homosexuals). And, although each case is different, each person individual, through all is a searching for self-identity and self-fulfillment to the utmost of the person's ability.

Consider the stereotyped "box" most women in this country are placed in from birth: that of becoming wife and mother, nothing else. Consider then, the girl brought up in this box who finds her sexual identification to be Lesbian. How then express the "wife-and-mother" role? This conflict often starts the process of self-searching which goes on for years and which, for some, is never resolved.

Toward a Quaker View of Sex, which came out of England and is more enlightened than most religious treatises on male homosexuality, fails utterly in its chapter on the female homosexual. The only statement with which we can agree is the first sentence: "Homosexuality is probably as common in women as it is in men." The Quaker view of the Lesbian is apparently that of the wishy-washy, namby-pamby old maid who holds hands with another old maid (or preferably an adoring younger girl, if available) because she never was able to catch a man and fulfill her deep yearning for the rewards of the pangs of childbirth. At least the American stereotype of the predatory, aggressive masculine woman has a little more color!

The Quaker view indicates that woman's prime requisite is her "maternal tenderness," that her only reason for being is to have babies, and that the Lesbian is warped and frustrated because she isn't doing her fair share toward the population explosion. To this question of maternity we must point out that the mere possession of biological machinery to produce babies has no correlation whatever with the attributes of motherhood. Let's face it—many women can have babies but make lousy mothers.

The art of motherhood in the human species is not instinctual. It is learned. We have courses in the care of the baby, and there are countless books on the market to help the young mother with the problems she may encounter during the course of her child's growth and development. In some cultures, babies are taken from the mothers and raised by the community without any apparent psychically traumatic results for the biological mothers or their offspring. In other cultures it is the male who tends the young.

It simply does not follow, then, that every Lesbian is suffering untold qualms because she is frustrating her "natural" birthright for giving birth. There are many other ways for women to contribute creatively to society, and at this particular point in the history of the population of our globe, they may also be highly desirable. The Lesbian who does feel frustrated because she doesn't have any children of her own may work in the teaching profession, she may be a playground director or a social worker who comes in contact with families and children. But the majority of Lesbians we have known have not expressed in any way the "void" they feel because they have no children. To the contrary, the expression, "I would prefer to lead a heterosexual life if I could," is much more apt to come from the male homosexual than from the female.

It must be said, however, that there are many Lesbians who are raising children—some successfully, some not so successfully. The rate of success is, of course, determined by the degree of self-acceptance and self-assurance of the mother, and the permanence and stability of her relationship to her Lesbian partner. It takes guts, grit and determination. For if a mother is determined to be a Lesbian the courts will assume she is an "unfit mother" on the face of it and take her children away from her. It seems children must have the protection of heterosexuals, regardless. The fact that *all homosexuals are products of heterosexuality* seems to escape those who would judge the homosexual relationship.

The teenage Lesbian has a particular problem which has not been met. Homophile organizations, like the Daughters of Bilitis, have had to refuse membership to those under 21 for fear that they will be charged with "contributing to the delinquency of a minor." The teenager has no one to turn to. Society thinks only in terms of counseling of the variety that would tend toward reestablishing the sexual identity in a heterosexual vein, and the teenage Lesbian is whisked off by her parents to the family doctor or clergyman to put a stop to this nonsense. However, in the cases that have come to our attention, the teenager has no doubt about her sexual orientation. What she wants to know is what to do about it. She wants to meet others like herself; she wants to socialize and to discuss the problems she faces. She is looking for Lesbian models, those who have worked out their problems and have established long-term relationships.

When she is denied this social outlet, she very often winds up in unsavory areas of a city like the Tenderloin in San Francisco. There she may find other youth, but she also finds herself in the company of prostitutes, pimps, drug addicts and dope peddlers. There have been several attempts in various cities to set up coffee houses where there is dancing for the teenage homosexual. But they have lacked the influential backing of, say, the church, to provide protection against police harassment while creating a wholesome social fabric for the teenage homosexual.

Because of the absence of role models in working out her way of life, and because the only marriage she has known is that of Mom and Dad, the young Lesbian usually gets hung up in the "butch-femme" syndrome in her early relationships. It is only with painful experience that she learns the Lesbian is attracted to a woman—not a cheap imitation of a man. The lasting Lesbian liaison (and there are many) is one based on mutuality of concern, love, companionship, responsibility, household chores, outside interests and sex.

The successful Lesbian relationship cannot be based on society's exaggerated male-female, dominant-passive roles, as depicted in the flood of Lesbian novels on the newsstands which are, for the most part, written by men for heterosexual male consumption. It is the realization that, contrary to cultural myths, all human beings have both feminine and masculine traits and that a person has to find her own identity as a woman and as a partner in this love relationship that makes for success. The fact that Lesbian relationships are generally long-lasting without benefit of religious ceremony or legal sanction is indicative of a strong bond of love and respect which sees the couple through all the obstacles society places in their way.

Fortunately for all women, there is a growing awareness in this country that woman needs and is more openly demanding an identity for herself as a human being, an identity over and beyond the societal role of housewife and mother. This awareness, coupled with more openness about sexuality and homosexuality, is making it easier now for the young girl, newly aware of her Lesbianism, to cope with the negative sanctions of society. But it is still true that in most areas of our country she has no place to turn for counsel, no one with whom she can talk about her feelings without running the very real risk that the counselor will turn away from her with horror and revulsion.

The Quakers state: "Female homosexuality is free from the legal and, to a large extent, the social sanctions which are so important in the problems of male homosexuals." This is a myth that even the male homosexual has come to believe. It is true that in England there were never any laws pertaining to female homosexuality. But this is not true in the U.S.A. The Lesbian is just as subject to the sanctions of certain laws as the male homosexual; she is just as subject to arrest when she sets foot in a "gay bar"; she is just as subject to blackmail and police harassment. The stigma attached to homosexuality has just as much effect on the Lesbian as she tries to deal with fear and society-imposed guilt in the problem areas of employment, family relationships and religion. Just because the record of arrests is so much smaller is no indication that the Lesbian is relatively free from legal or social sanction. It only means that she is less obvious and less promiscuous. She has done a better job of covering up.

Lesbian problems we have dealt with over the years include the 20-year-old driven to thoughts of suicide because she could not resolve the conflict between her identity as a Lesbian and as a Christian. Or the 40-year-old mother who telephoned Daughters of Bilitis 3,000 miles across the country to break "18 years of silence" after reading a book called *The Grapevine* by Jess Stearn. Then there was the nurse with a "perfect work record" in a federal hospital who was interrogated by a government investigator, flown from Washington, D.C., at the taxpayers' expense, because someone wrote to a Congressman accusing her of being a Lesbian.

There was the 19-year-old who was trying to find out what homosexuality was all about because she was drummed out of the armed services on a charge she didn't understand. The daughter who receives a monthly allowance from her wealthy family in the Midwest to stay on the coast lest her district attorney father be threatened with a "family skeleton" by his political foes. And the 25-year-old who, after five years of psychiatric therapy, decides she must make the best of herself as herself—a Lesbian.

The most serious problem a Lesbian faces in life is that of self-acceptance. Like everyone else, she has been taught the cultural folklore that a Lesbian is something less than human—a sick, perverted, illegal, immoral animal to be shunned and despised. Needless to say, with the first glimmering of self-knowledge, of awareness that she has Lesbian tendencies, she becomes bogged down in doubt, fear, guilt and hostility.

Some Lesbians claim they have been aware of their Lesbianism since early childhood. Others first become aware during adolescence. Yet there are some women who make this discovery about themselves much later in life—after they have been married and have had children. Still others, either by choice or lack of opportunity, never admit or act out their Lesbianism.

It isn't easy for a woman to say to herself, let alone anyone else, "I am a Lesbian." But once the words are said, has she really changed? Isn't she still the same person she was—the dear friend, the competent employee, the loving sister? And yet the words become a barrier in her personal and working relationships. To protect her family and her job, she is forced to live a lie, to take on a dual life. No wonder many Lesbians seek out some type of psychiatric or therapeutic help. The miracle is that so many are able to function so well and to contribute so much to society.

The Lesbian is thus a secretive, chameleon creature. She is not easily recognized. The old adage, "It takes one to know one," is not true. Not being distinguishable from other women, she has difficulty meeting others like herself. The "gay bar" is still a meeting place, but there are few such bars which cater to women exclusively because they do not constitute a steady clientele. Besides, a Lesbian, as a woman, has no doubt heard many times the old saw "nice girls don't go into bars," or "no lady would ever go into a bar alone." The Lesbian goes out on the town only occasionally and is more apt to settle down with a partner, to build a home and a lasting relationship, and to develop a small circle of friends—usually both homosexual and heterosexual. Another social outlet for the Lesbian can be homophile organizations throughout the country (if she knows about them), such as Daughters of Bilitis, which has chapters in New York and San Francisco.

The Lesbian, being a woman, comes out of the same cultural pool as do heterosexual women. Therefore, on top of everything else, she may have the same hang-ups and inhibitions about sex, dress, work, actions, etc., as do her heterosexual sisters. Since women have been taught to be passive, to shun the role of the aggressor, the Lesbian finds herself without the slightest idea of how to approach another woman for a date, for a conversation, for sex. It is a rarity for a heterosexual woman to be approached by a Lesbian unless she has given much indication that such advances are welcome.

Even when the Lesbian accepts her sexual identity and herself as a person, she still faces very real discrimination from society. If she has educated herself to a profession (a role doubly difficult for any woman), she can lose her professional status merely because someone points a finger. This is especially true of teachers, attorneys, doctors, social workers and other professions licensed by the state. But it can also be true for file clerks and secretaries. Very few employers are aware enough to realize that in the Lesbian he has an employee who must work, who will not get married or pregnant, who will devote her energies and capabilities to her job because she will always have to support herself.

As Rabbi Elliot Grafman has stated, "People fear that which they do not understand, and what they fear they despise." It is only through more knowledge and more personal confrontation that the stereotype of the Lesbian can be dispelled. However, to accomplish this feat is to overcome the vicious circle that now envelops the Lesbian who tries to be honest.

If she divulges her identity, she automatically becomes vulnerable. She faces loss of job, family and friends. Yet, until she opens herself to such possibilities, no one will have the opportunity to come to know and to understand her as the whole person she is.

Through The Council on Religion and the Homosexual, which was formed in San Francisco in 1964 after a three-day retreat attended by clergymen and male and female representatives of the homophile community, such a dialogue began in earnest. Avenues of communication have been opened up not only with the religious community (seminaries and other church groups), but with governmental agencies, the police, business and professional groups, college and high school students. But the task of demythologizing, of education and redefinition of the homosexual is a long and arduous one.

To My Friend Miriam

By Martha Shelley

She was never athletic,
yet by sitting still,
tensed for a shower of blows
her shoulders had secreted muscle.

Never the schoolgirl of unconscious grace,
not the fair-haired leader
most certainly not the sweetheart of Sigma Chi—
she had acquired a tough butch rep of late;
cross between a casanova and a hood—
and half believed in it herself.

So I was surprised,
but most of all she was surprised
to know that she had been beside a fire,
beside a woman, drinking wine,
talking, unable to reach for a waiting hand;
talking until it became absurdly late,
and they retired in polite dismay
to separate rooms.

♀ The March-April double issue on Women's Liberation is truly superb. Such an issue has been long overdue as has the awakening among women all over the country with regard to their own oppression and need for liberation. My interest in the WLM stems primarily from an existential realization and joy over the fact that it isn't merely a reformist or an anti-male or a "let's be men" movement, but one deeply concerned about and moving toward radically new life styles and humane attitudes. The liberation of women is also the liberation of men. Just as blacks have had to learn, let women also learn to shout again and again, "Say it out loud—I'm woman and proud!"

Ames, Iowa

♀ *Yes,* this is the end of *my* subscription and of many others from my home church. Many of your issues have been most disgusting, but the March-April one was absolutely the most insulting piece of trash that I have ever had in my hands. I feel that you are undermining the very foundation of our homes and churches and therefore the nation. We are reminded that if the communists can destroy the structure of our homes, their job of destroying our society is well on the way to establishment. Being a wife and mother is a lovely and beautiful life and just whom do you want to "Liberate" and for what?

Richmond, Virginia

♂ In the middle of the night, I secreted myself in a dark shower stall with penlight in hand to read the editorials and articles on the pitiful plight of the girls. Deep, dark forebodings beset me as to what might happen if my Rebecca got hold of the issue; poor lass—four kids, 100% female, and swears she wouldn't trade me as a playmate for the best Lesbian in town. Just doesn't understand the situation, I guess.

It is apparent that your writers, at least, are prepared to accept socially all sorts of deviates without a trace of stigma. If they aren't careful, they may become so permissive that they accept "normal people," or worse, even conservatives! Perish the thought!

My honest reaction to such hogwash is that your gals who write it have spent too much time contemplating their navel.

Lubbock, Texas

♀ I have just read that the May issue of *motive* has had its publication postponed. I was sorry to read of this. Certainly the "four-letter words" used in the March-April issue were not out of place, especially with the excellent explanation given for their use in the editorial. Of course I do not know all the facts, but if the postponement has to do with the use of "four-letter words" in the manner of the March-April issue or is in some way connected with the content of that issue, then I must protest!

Certainly The Methodist Church and its officials have more important things to do than hassle over "four-letter words," especially when male chauvinism is so rampant in The Methodist Church itself. When our denomination has been ordaining women since 1956, how can it still make recruiting films called "It Takes a Man"? Why do most of the official forms still ask for 'wife's name' instead of 'spouse's name'; and why does the Discipline continually refer to 'the minister and his wife' rather than 'the minister and spouse'? Why is no recruiting for the parish ministry done among women? I did not even know that it was possible for a woman to be a parish minister until I got to seminary. However, seminaries are no exception, for it is my seminary experience so far that has convinced me of just how deep the prejudice against women is. The March-April issue of *motive* is a ray of light.

Boston, Massachusetts

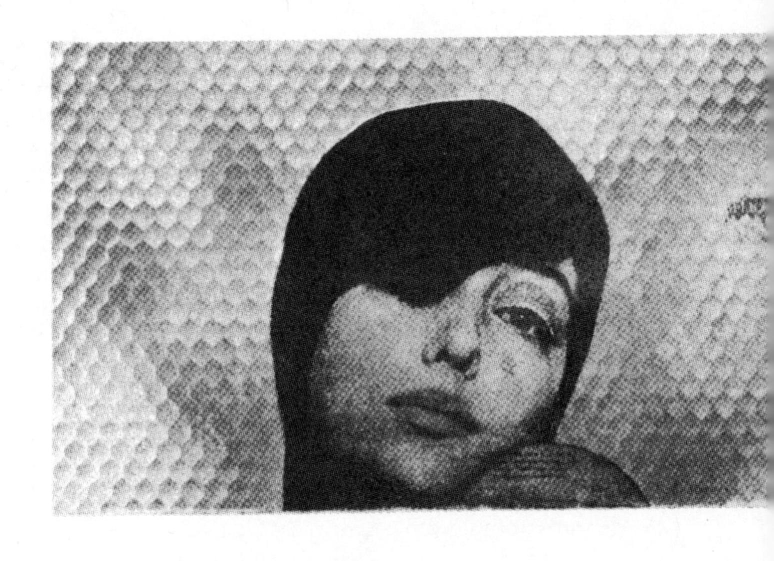

♀ ——— **Woman**

As

Secretary

Sexpot

Spender

Sow

Civic Actor

Sickie

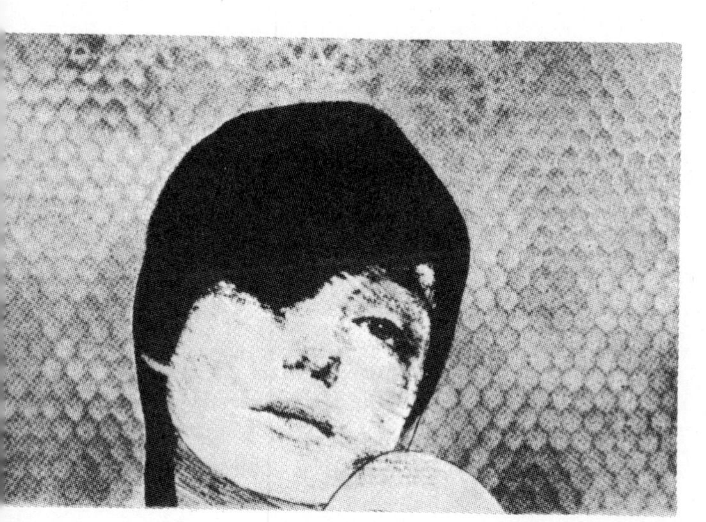

LITHOGRAPH: A FACE TO GLOW
WITH EVERY FASHION
George Miyasaki

I have a Bachelor's degree in French literature. The smartest thing I ever did, however, was to take a typing course my junior year in high school; without it I would never be able to find a job. (secretary, age 24)

Ever since I had Kevin I lie in bed at night and plan what I'm going to do the next day. When I need to go to the drugstore to buy some more Pampers, that's a big thing. I plan my whole day around it. I can't believe that's

By Marilyn Salzman Webb 

become an excursion out for me now. (new mother, age 21, college graduate)

Ye gods—what do I do (all day)? Well, I get up and out of bed at 6 A.M. I get my son dressed and then get breakfast. After breakfast I wash dishes, then bathe and feed my baby. She's 3 months old. Then I start the procedure of house cleaning. I make beds, dust, mop, sweep, vacuum. Then I do my baby's wash. Then I get lunch for the three of us. Then I put my baby to bed, and the little boy to bed for his nap. Then I usually sew or mend or wash windows or iron and do the things I can't possibly get done before noon. Then I cook supper for my family. After supper my husband usually watches TV while I wash dishes. I get the kids to bed. Then—if I'm lucky—I'm able to sit down, watch TV or read a magazine. Then I set my hair and go to bed. (a 22-year-old housewife, quoted in Workingman's Wife, *p. 34)*

"Take her off the stage and fuck her," was the polite greeting of a "radical" brother as one woman tried to speak about the Women's Liberation Movement recently. "Go home; women have it good in our society." Sadly, that just isn't true!

Our Women's Liberation group in Washington, D. C., has been concerned with the emptiness of women's lives. We've looked at ads, heard the personal testimonies, and tried to understand why we all, in one way or another, have lived alone and isolated, keeping those stories of our days locked up inside. How did we come to this situation; why do we live depersonalized, dehumanized existences? How does society reinforce this emptiness?

Through months of talk, study and reflection, we have come to the understanding that we, as women, are brought up to behave in specific ways. We are trained for particular roles in this society, and we are given very few alternatives. We label these roles Secretary, Sexpot, Sow, Spender, Civic Actor and Sickie. Each role reinforces the others, but they are all interrelated. Spender is a function of all the others, while Sickie is their failure. All of them are limiting and dehumanizing to us as thinking, feeling human beings.

Why, if these roles are limited and dehumanizing, have they been perpetuated? It would be easy simply to see men as the immediate enemy and the cause of women's oppression; yet this would imply that the cause is rooted in something inherently evil in men. It is necessary, therefore, to look into the present social system and to examine how, over a long period of time, society programs people, men and women, into specific roles that fit its needs for maintaining itself.

Social order grows out of basic human needs. In early human history, these needs were quite simple: food, shelter, and physical protection. To survive, ancient humans devised ways to care for themselves, creating simple forms of social organization to meet these basic needs. As methods for meeting basic needs became more sophisticated, social organization changed to adapt most efficiently to changes in methods of production.

In *Origins of the Family, Private Property and the State,* Engels describes the change from a primitive, communal society, with group marriage and collective work for collective ends, to a property-oriented, pairing social structure that developed class differentiations of work and life-style.

Tribes, Engels said, divided labor so that men cared for cattle and women maintained communal farms and cared for children and domestic chores. In this early period, there were no status differentiations between men's and women's work; both were necessary for survival, and both contributed to the good of the whole community.

Then early forms of trading began. Cattle became the early

unit of exchange around which all other forms of trade were measured. Trade broke down the concept of work for the necessity of the community, and developed the notions of bartering and property. If one could trade something for something else, one owned what one traded. Since cattle, which was the assigned responsibility of men, became the unit of trade, it followed that men became the first owners of property. This subtle shift spelled the end of communal production and the beginning of private wealth vested in the hands of men.

Property owned by men could not be passed to their sons if paternity was uncertain. Thus the economic development of trade slowly changed the family structure from a kind of group commune to pairing and marriage. Whereas before, sexual relations were free and open within the group, now strict fidelity was demanded to insure known paternity and thus heredity lineage. Women became, like cattle, the property of men.

Several groups or classes emerged: those men who owned cattle, and those who did not. Secondary to this were women who were the property of either the owners or the laborers. The wealthy began to live differently from the workers; they developed sports and "refined" tastes, engaged in wars and consumed the products of others' work. The workers engaged in arduous drudgery with no leisure time and no energy for anything more than survival. Religions and customs developed which reinforced this emerging class society.

Marx emphasizes that the superstructure of society develops around the economic base, or the means of production. There is cultural lag; customs may carry over even after the previous productive form has been outdated; but those who adapt most quickly to new forms of production develop a new social organization that reflects that new economy. The owners of this new productive form thus gain the power to define, by providing the means by which others can survive, how social organization will develop.

Our own history and our own society today reflect the power of the productive process to define us in our guts. American women are used for profits, and we are programmed to make our capitalist system run most effectively for the good of those who reap the benefits of our work.

Quite early, London merchants who put money into the "new world" realized that men alone would not build a stable colony, but would remain shifting adventurists unless women could be provided to settle them down. In 1619 they sent "Agreeable persons, young and incorrupt . . . sold with their own consent to settlers as wives, the price to be the cost of their own transportations." (Flexner, p. 3)

These women, and the many more who came, either by being kidnapped in England, or in search of a husband, or by selling themselves as indentured servants, became, like slaves, the property of the men they lived with. In marriage, they had few civil rights; they, like slaves, did not exist as human beings under law. They were expected to behave with deference and obedience; they had little education and were expected to breed and to do their share of the work.

The patriarchal extended family was the basic social and economic unit. All goods the family used were produced by its members; and work was divided so that women cared for the house and farmyard, while men brought home lumber, meat, grain and wool. The house was a small factory that employed old men, women and children and produced all the family needed.

With the invention of the spinning jenny, the power loom and other industrial machines, and with a rising demand for mass-produced items, a new era in American production began. Women who saw their lives waning under the thumb of men at home flocked to the new mills to gain some economic independence and freedom.

> Mass production made it easier and often cheaper to purchase the family's needs than to rely on home production. This meant that the family's greatest need was *cash* income to buy processed foods and manufactured goods. Because the new factory system needed workers, women and even children were encouraged to seek employment. (Wells, p. 4)

But "freedom" to work and to leave the demanding private family unit was deceptive. Factories merely moved hard labor from the home to the central workplace, and made money for the mill owners, while the workers were still impoverished.

Since the typical workday for the factory girl lasted from sunup (4:30 A.M.) to sundown, it completely altered family relationships. Workers had only a few short hours together, and they had to live within textile villages that were entirely run and owned by the factory. Single women, whose wages were always lower than men's, earned from $1 to $3 per week, out of which they had to pay $1.50 to $1.75 for board in the company-owned houses. Economic freedom did not appear, and the living conditions of workers grew steadily worse.

Expanded industry created a new middle class and freed growing numbers of women from domestic drudgery, giving them time to work in new "service" occupations. The Civil War (wars always being times when women are enlisted to take on the work of fighting men) opened up new economic roles for women. They began teaching and hospital work and, with the invention of the typewriter in 1867, they entered new clerical fields.

Although two world wars have changed the situation for short periods, women have remained in the same occupations they held before World War I. They did clerical and factory work and they continuously expanded the new "soothing" professions like social work, nursing, and teaching. Propaganda and mass mobilizations for the "war effort" got women to fill in while men fought, but they were quickly sent home again when the men returned.

Without a whimper, women believed what they were told and followed the needs of a changing economy. When women were wanted during World War II, companies provided child care facilities; when the male workers returned, there were no more child care programs. Social scientists were popularized who maintained that motherhood was a full-time, all-important job. Freud was useful in the process, as were Margaret Mead and the functional sociologists who eulogized that what existed was good.

As capitalism became more sophisticated and further rationalized, it demanded that other values replace these. Early competitive capitalism was consolidated by growing monopolies and large corporate conglomerates.

The corporation has replaced the old family structure and early competitive small business around which community was organized and socialization occurred. A new corporation man or woman must learn to work collectively in each corporation for the profit of that firm. He must repress bald competitive urges and fit smoothly into his niche in a well-oiled machine geared for maximum efficiency. He must find outlets for his tension in situations other than the workplace. Here we see the ultimate form of personal adaptation, defined by the productive process for the higher profits of some and the survival of the rest.

But the development of the productive corporation and the corporate personality isn't by any means the whole story. At the turn of the century, in his search for new markets, Henry Ford discovered that if he paid his workers more than the bare minimum for survival, they could afford his automobiles. They could be markets as well as workers to maximize his profits. The consumption economy had deep roots in the past; the rich had always consumed in quantity. But the notion of the mass market appeared only at the turn of the century. The gearing up for the sales effort began, and it has since become one of modern capitalism's nerve centers.

Thus the advertising industry arose, first to announce new products, then to convince the prospective buyer of the absolute necessity of the product, and finally to encourage waste consumption.

Since society demands that woman's place be in the home, her economic function easily became that of consumer; each household was seen as both a production and a consumption unit.

> Nothing makes markets like a marriage. There's new business in setting up house, and future business in raising a family. All together it's big business, appliances and house furnishings to stepped-up insurance and bigger cars. (*New York Times* ad for *TV Guide*, Nov. 6, 1968)

Today the advertising promotion and sales business eats up most of the spending of large corporations. Baran and Sweezy estimate that expenditures for sales efforts, if market research, public relations and commercial design are included, had reached the phenomenal figure of over $20 billion by 1966. Corporate workers were complaining that the sales departments were taking over business by reaching back into design and product development to maximize product turnover.

This sales effort fit in nicely with the developing corporate and worker personalities. As workers had to suppress their human tensions, both physically and mentally, and as feelings of powerlessness grew in the face of ever-expanding economic conglomerates and political manipulations, people came to see purchasing power as their only outlet for freedom of choice. Trends of mass consumption culture were set by an elite leisure class that had fostered the myth of the American Dream where "anyman" could be a success and live surrounded by cars and appliances. Conspicuous consumption clouded the class nature of American society and allowed a worker to feel he had it made when he could buy a TV and lounge in his prefabricated backyard.

In middle-class America, "the duties of vicarious leisure and consumption devolve upon the wife alone . . . for the good name of the household." (Veblen, p. 68) She is the ceremonial consumer of goods which the husband produces. Her dress, her household goods, her "refinement," her ladylikeness and "culture" are symbolic of the household's ability to pay. Her job is to expand the consumption economy and to reinforce the American Dream.

If the economy needed people to consume, and if the mark of success were to be set by the "style" of the rich in which women played the role of an expensive mannequin of leisure culture, and if the economy needed women to stay at home and reduce the pressures of unemployment, it followed that popular culture would proclaim women's fashions and products for the home to be key concerns of the American woman. The statistics show that we have listened well: during the '60's there was a massive boom in consumer goods, particularly clothing and household commodities. Women make 75% of all consumer purchases.

Secretary

Twenty-eight million women now work in America. They work in almost every job listed by the Bureau of the Census, but contrary to a now popular ad, "you have *not* come a long way, baby." Most women are employed in the same occupations we've had for centuries. We do the crap work of society!

Clerical work is the largest single occupation of women workers. In 1960, thirty-one percent of all women who worked were secretaries, bookkeepers, stenographers, and clerk-typists.

The next largest occupation of women is service work—over fifteen percent of working women are waitresses, cooks, bartenders, and hospital attendants, not including nurses. In 1960, two out of three women in the service category were waitresses, and most of the jobs in this category were only part-time.

Fourteen percent of women workers do factory work—they are operators, assemblers, and other kindred workers, always with wages lower than those of men. We are the first fired and the last hired. Blacks get more attention than we do.

Slightly over thirteen percent of us are professionals. Forty-two percent of all professionals were teachers (except college) in 1965, and seven out of ten of these teachers taught in elementary schools. Since then, secondary schools and junior high schools have become even more the domain of men.

One-fourth of the professionals were in the health professions, the largest single occupation being nursing, followed by dental and medical technicians. ". . . Women hold only a small proportion of the positions as engineers, technicians (other than medical and dental) and scientists, despite the numerous job openings created by the tremendous interest in research and development." (*Handbook on Women Workers,* p. 95)

In 1963, over sixty percent of those women who had earned BA's in 1958 were classified as full-time housewives: they held no job at all. The statistics further indicate that even if we weren't working as housewives and wanted to work, our preparation was not the best for professions other than those listed above.

Forty-three percent of us majored in education in the school year 1963–64. Twenty-two percent were in the humanities and the arts; fourteen percent were in social sciences. We aren't given much on-the-job training in comparison to men with BAs. They give us a typing test and men a management training test when we look for jobs straight out of college.

The prospects for us as workers aren't good. The earning gap between men and women has widened continually. In 1964, the median income of male workers was $6,283; for female workers it was $3,710.

Women's jobs are usually part-time, so real earnings are further decreased since we aren't given fringe benefits like health and life insurance plans given full-time male workers.

Furthermore, not only have we stagnated in "women's vocations," we have regressed. In 1940, forty percent of all working women worked in service jobs; today that figure has reached fifty-four percent. Plus there has been a decline in the percent of women professionals with PhDs, since 1930. We have greater unemployment than men even when we are the sole support of our families, and that is very often. Forty-two percent of working women support themselves and others, and an additional twenty-four percent have husbands who earn less than $5,000 a year.

How did we get in this position? How did we get the scutwork of society? We have been placed in the lowest paying, lowest skilled, and most boring jobs in America, a country overburdened with boring jobs anyway, by workforce *channeling!*

> The fact is that the 'woman's place is in the home' myth is a phony rationalization for paying lower wages and providing worse working conditions for women than men . . . (Employers) use the feminine mystique to mold women into 'their place' in industry, the place of the reserve labor pool. They can be thrown in or out of the labor market at will, used as part-time or temporary workers, kept in the lowest-paying jobs with a minimum of resistance, and their rate of exploitation is the highest (women have lower median income than black people). (Wells, p. 9)

Our media, education, families, in fact our entire socialization is for this channeling in adult life. "You are nobody unless you marry"—love comics tell you that all the time. "You are a poor housewife and mother unless you buy things"—magazines just assume that. "You are to be pretty, not as smart as men, sexy, and not compete with men in any way." "Your job will fit into what is feminine and ladylike—it is innate, you know, that women love kids."

Sexpot

"Ain't she sweet
Makin' profit off her meat.
She's just America's prime commodity.
Ain't she sweet."

(SUNG BY WOMEN'S LIBERATION AT THE MISS AMERICA PAGEANT, 1968

We are to entertain men; we are the playgirls of America. One lucky girl each month makes it into *Playboy's* centerfold, but each of us wants to be there and to be the Myth America of every man's dreams.

From the prostitute to the advertising model to the socialite hostess, women have been able to make it in life by selling their sexiness. We have been made to see our bodies as commodities. We are to entertain men and to sell products—use your bod, kid, not your mind.

Besides the more blatant sex-roles of the call girls, we serve as sex entertainers in many other jobs, such as airline stewardesses (United's flight's "for men only") or special receptionists ("Hertz has one leg up on Detroit."). Katherine Gibbs' high class secretarial schools teach girls to dress to be expensive-looking in a luxury office.

Sex sells everything from cigarettes to farm machinery, and it sells "beauty products" to maintain the image. "The call of the Wild Streak: It's irresistible. Now! The first complete kit to fashion-streak your hair. Like all good lures, the Wild Streak by Clairol is beautifully simple. No retouching for up to six seductive months. Why hide the secret siren inside of you? Answer the call of the Wild Streak. You're not the type to be timid. And this is no time to be tame." (*Cosmopolitan,* the sex seller of them all.)

Get it? Women are to be screwed and not heard. That's part of it. The other part is that they're to buy all the products they can afford to make sure they are desirable enough to get a man.

> A good housewife knows how to be an expensive mistress. Are you so busy being devoted to your husband you never make reckless demands? That's a mistake! Try acting spoiled now and then. Simply have to have some wildly beautiful extravagance. This extraordinary Natural Russian Crown Sable should fill the bill admirably. How will your husband feel about suddenly having an expensive mistress? He'll complain about the cost of maintenance. And he'll be a lot more attentive. (*New York Times* ad, Nov. 24, 1968)

This ad, to sell an air conditioning system, in *Fortune* magazine, the Bible of Big Business, speaks for itself.

> "What a way to heat your building," said above two men taking off their glasses to look at a new miniskirted secretary. "Miss Johnson is a warm-blooded animal. Her thermostat is set at 98.6°. She burns food and generates a lot of heat. So much, in fact, that she and her co-workers overheat modern, tightly insulated buildings and cause the air conditioning to turn on. Even when it's cold outside . . ." (So these guys sell spot air conditioning to cool areas where all the hot chicks are, so to speak.)

You can find others in every magazine, but the point is that the selling we do is billion dollar business. The buying we do to keep up the sexual sell is even higher. It's American business, patriotic and a sure way to whip up marriage consumer units. "Here, kids, try this. The first one's free." We are the woman behind the great man. We are the whore of American Capitalism!

And whore we become to society if we give in. Many men view sex as freeing women—that is, if we are free with sex we are truly liberated, and our identity problems are gone. *Playboy* proclaimed "The New Girl" in one of its recent issues. She is "unabashedly sexy, charmingly individualistic, and a joy to the men in her life." They make us feel that we will be loved if we screw; that's what all our sexual gearing up is supposed to be for—or is it?

Society on the surface keeps sex under the cover—literally. We don't talk about it; it's dirty. Because we've made it a commodity, we've also made love a commodity, along with beauty, trust, and human interrelatedness. If we're discreet, that's ok, but God help the woman who gets herself pregnant. Then she's treated like the whore people thought she was all along. Over 10,000 women each year, at lowest estimates, have abortions. Most of these are illegal, done in some doctor's office, if the girl is lucky, and in some hotel room or rundown tenement, if she's not. Whole institutions are built up around unwanted pregnancies—isolated homes for a woman "to go on vacation" for nine months, abandoned children's homes, etc. We are left to make it alone or die; society could care less.

Birth control information is kept a dark secret for most women. Only if she's black or poor is it pushed; then for rather hazy reasons that often resemble genocide. Teenage girls cannot get birth control devices in most cities. Unless you are married or engaged, most college clinics will not help you out, either.

Spender

And so we buy to make ourselves appealing, to get a husband 'cause that man in our life will presumably give the emptiness meaning.

Properly manipulated (if you're not afraid of that word), American housewives can be given the sense of purpose, creativity, identity, the self-realization, even the sexual joy they lack—by buying things. (So proclaims an ad executive Betty Friedan interviewed.)

Department stores are the Broadway shows and the circuses of the American housewife. A shopping trip is an excursion into fantasy, a relief from vacuuming and diaper-changing, a chance to get dressed up and spend a day without the kids. It is a pacifier for powerlessness, a chance to choose one of many identical brands of toothpaste and pretty bathroom tissues. We hope our new pantsuit will get us the attention, the love, the security that life has robbed from us. It's a very pretty system that saps our human potential and adds to the gross national product.

Fortune magazine predicts consumers will spend over $36 billion for fashion goods this coming year. They further say that consumer outlays for fashion goods have risen by $15 billion or forty percent in the past four years, a rise equal to the last fifteen years put together. Home goods sales have risen $11 billion in the same period. Consumer purchases have been eating up greater percentages of disposable income (income after necessities are satisfied) yearly.

Capitalism hasn't yet been able to devise a well-planned system for workers to buy back the products they produce. It has thus created the system of credit and installment buying, so that products can move from factory to home, leaving the burden of forking up the money with the little guy. Besides, it makes bank profits—those big guys stick together.

Today over twenty-one percent of the average family's income is used to pay back installments, mortgages, personal loans and other consumer debts. Consumer debt has risen at a fantastic rate in this same period. In 1950, $14 billion in installment and consumer credit was "spent." By 1966, this figure was up to $74 billion.

Since women spend the major amount of this money, it is clear they have us going in the right direction for their purposes, but we've been selling our souls to the company stores.

Before a girl marries, she buys. Major and small appliances. Living, dining and bedroom furniture. A TV set. Rugs and carpeting. China. Silver. Linens. Draperies. Household furnishings of every description. She must buy them. She's moving into her first home—an empty house or apartment. (The ad tells American Business to advertise in *Modern Bride Magazine*—the magazine that sells it to unsuspecting newlyweds.)

Sow

Our programmed role of housewife and mother helps them hold us up for the sales. We creatively redecorate our homes to provide sanctuary for our men who hate their jobs, or to lure them back if they are among the few who find total escape in their work. We learn to see our lives in terms of others—our kids will have it better than we, our husbands are winning us social status no single girl could have.

Marriage is a property relationship. Kids are the products we produce; if we fail with them, we are no good. So we'd better make motherhood a full-time profession, smother them with love and toys or we will fail for sure.

The economy plays on this insecurity about motherhood. The youth market, according to *Business Week,* is now worth $15 billion a year, just for teenagers alone. As allowances went up, with the family's disposable income, advertisers began to appeal directly to youth to exercise their newly found freedom by buying. Parents are pressured to raise allowances, as well as to buy toys and new foods for smaller children, who are counted on by TV advertisers to push their parents to buy. No part of the family is sacred to the advertisers, and Mommy is made to buy, not only for herself but for every member of the family.

Family relationships are put under severe strain. The husband has to earn enough to keep up with and to surpass the Joneses. His wife has to soothe him to help him regain the confidence and identity that are destroyed by his dehumanizing office or factory job. She must produce "beautiful children" who do well in school and who don't become delinquents, hippies, or—horror of horrors—commie protesters. She has to look pretty, on top of all her domestic drudgery, to keep a good image for the family and to keep her man by being the expensive mistress he might otherwise seek.

It's no wonder relationships collapse; but even the collapse is now a commodity. An ad for Sony TV reads, "It's nice to be alone with the one you love." It shows a man and a woman in bed, facing opposite directions watching different programs on their little, private TV's. They're wearing earphones so as not to disturb the continuity of the corporate message with extraneous noise—like talk, perhaps?

Civic Actor

So what can homebound mothers do besides buy? If we're disturbed about America, or if we want some stimulation and interest outside the home, we can join the PTA, the church, the League of Women Voters, or volunteer to help retarded children. If we want a change, we can join an organization that will pressure Congress or elect a candidate. That's important for women to do—after all, we are fifty-three percent of the population. Civic affairs is now the great American pacifier, second only to consumption. It rests on the myth that power and decision-making are accessible in this country.

Political scientists want us to believe that we live in a pluralistic society. If one wants change, one organizes a pressure group strong enough to effect that change. That's democracy!

But real power doesn't lie with the state, Congress, the courts or pressure groups. The power that counts—the power to define how the rest will work and live—lies with private corporations. Their assumptions about economic growth determine how production will occur, and they define how we all work and live. This is *the* central decision.

C. Wright Mills describes the system this way:

> There is no effective countervailing power against the coalition of the big businessmen—who as political outsiders, now occupy the command posts—and the ascendant military men—who with such grave voices now speak so frequently in the higher councils. (*The Power Elite,* Mills, p. 267)

Even John Kenneth Galbraith, that stalwart of American "liberalism," knows where it's at.

> The industrial system . . . is inextricably associated with the state. In notable respects the mature corporation is an arm of the state. And the state, in important matters, is an instrument of the industrial system. (*The New Industrial State,* p. 296)

Galbraith demonstrates the common practice for corporate executives and millionaires to move in and out of government at top administrative and decision-making levels. The permanent establishment of the military and the growth of the aerospace and defense industry were not coincidental.

> The mature corporation . . . depends on the state for trained manpower, the regulation of aggregate demands for stability in wages and price. . . . The state, through military and other technical procurements, underwrites the corporation's largest capital commitments in its area of most advanced technology. (p. 308)

The state trains corporate manpower, gives fat contracts for corporate development, and makes damn sure national and international policy help corporate growth. Talk about socialism, the rich have it for sure. The state and the corporation are usually one and the same group of people changing caps every so often.

That the vote is meaningless was made most clear by this past presidential election. McCarthy supporters saw that even a candidate with popular support, shown in state primaries, had no way of breaking through the party structure to get the nomination. Most states did not even have primaries; and in many of those that did, it was not mandatory that delegations to the conventions support the primary election candidate. Local party structures are controlled not by us, but by those same men who speak for big business or who support it.

Wallace supporters saw that it was nearly impossible for any third party to win against the weight of entrenched look-alikes like the Democrats and Republicans.

The vote has been the biggest myth grabbed by the American people. Sure, we get to choose between two or even three candidates every few years, but elections don't let us decide on central political issues. Those decisions will be made privately, untouched even by public debate. Remember that Johnson, during the 1964 Presidential election, was the peace candidate, and that he won because voters were appalled as Goldwater promised escalation in Vietnam.

And what about Congress, that great representative voice of the people?

> . . . as social types, these (Congressmen) are not representative of the rank and file citizen. They represent those who have been successful in entrepreneurial and professional endeavors. Older men, they are of the privileged white, native-born, of native parents, Protestant Americans . . . They are, in short, in and of the new and old upper classes of local society. (Mills, p. 248)

Senator Gale McGee, on the Senate floor on Feb. 4, 1969, said:

> In the US Senate today there are said to be 27 millionaires. This is up from what it was two years ago, and that was up from the preceding election, and so on. My point is we are gradually forfeiting service in our National Congress to the millionaires. *(Congressional Record)*

And these are the campaigns women, as the majority of campaign workers, staff.

> More and more the fundamental issues never come to any point of decision before the Congress, or before its most powerful committees, much less before the electorate in campaigns. (Mills, p. 255)

No Congress ever declared war in Vietnam, and you can bet your next picket sign many Congressmen don't even know about the wars we are presently waging in Laos, Cambodia, Bolivia, Guatemala and Peru.

PTA's aren't any better. Business is glad for us to work for free to make for better schools. Better schools make better students who will become better workers—especially new white-collar workers who are now much in demand.

Forward together, we will create a more rationalized capitalism. Women—help staff nicer social institutions and keep up the image of citizen participation in democracy, but don't come near where real decisions are made. Remember, your place is in the home.

The Collapse of Roles: Sickie

When these roles fail to satisfy, as they do, women resort to the salves of all oppressed groups. They take to drugs and drink, and if they can afford it, to psychiatry.

Indices of rising drinking and drug use, let alone psychiatric care, show that during the last two decades American consumption has zoomed way ahead of any previous predictions.

Psychiatry, the art of fitting people back into their socially designated places, is expanding by leaps and bounds. New institutes, like Esalen, and new forms of therapy—dance, group, drug, Rogerian, etc.—are growing wildly and women flock to them to find some happiness and security.

A study now under way at George Washington University indicates that much larger proportions of women are on drugs and in psychiatric care than men.

Any society finds ways of dealing with its maladjusted, but never has a society seemed so maladjusted as ours. "Over one-half of all the hospital beds in this country are occupied by mental patients. There are 500,000 psychiatric patients housed in public and private mental hospitals at any given time." (Shofield, p. 4) This doesn't include the hordes of us going to local shrinks.

As of 1951, the World Health Organization estimated that the United States had the greatest number of alcoholics as a percent of total adult population in the world. Alcoholism and other drug use has risen sharply since that year.

Consider "crime." Taxpayers shell out over $12 million each day just on maintaining prison systems, and $4 billion annually for "law enforcement." That's higher, percentage-wise, than any other country in the world. This doesn't include the "welfare prison system," where women who are poor are subject to prying scrutiny in their homes all hours of the day. Many "criminals" are women—prostitutes unable to make a decent living elsewhere or forced into it by the system of sexual objectification.

Something is terribly wrong with this whole system—a system that forces us to conform or be labeled sick or locked up for "deviance."

Could it be that we have been programmed to self-destruct when our tolerance for living in this America gets very low? That is much better than the route of revolution, in the eyes of the corporate rulers and their professional "crisis managers."

It should be clear that the roles we see as our only alternatives in this society are quite essential to the continuation of the status quo. We fit in all too well. We continue to play these roles because we have learned them from childhood. We are afraid to be concerned about our condition for fear of being called frustrated, unsexy, feminist, communist, or other synonyms for bad. Because we have been brought up to think of ourselves as inferior, we block our minds and come to believe we are.

Remember the times in elementary school when girls were the smartest in the class? Somewhere between then and high school we learned that smartness doesn't pay off for our prime goal in life—that of getting and keeping a man, at least not the kind of smartness we learned in schools. We learned that girls with brains didn't have dates; that cheerleaders were the envy of all girls in the school. We learned to see each other as competitors for that all-important man, and to be wary of each other. That's how the programming began, but it got much more complex as we got older.

The roles we have described are functional to capitalism, whether or not women play them. Someone has to consume; someone has to be surplus labor with depressed wages. The system is capable of giving us as women a token of integration, just as it has begun to give blacks. We must not be misled by our new supposed freedoms. We must create a new society where no one has to play these roles, and where we, as women, can all develop to the highest of our human potential.

What shall we do?

Because we have been kept from each other, and because we are in the unique position of having to live a daily "desegregated" life with a representative of the system of male supremacy (a house slave, while we are field slaves), we must meet and organize for mutual support, solidarity and major social change.

We should have three main goals in mind:

One: To increase our understanding, from our own personal experiences, of the way in which we, as women, have been programmed and oppressed, and to analyze the social institutions that create the context of our oppression.

Two: To devise methods of changing our situation by changing the corporate economic structure so these roles are not necessary. We must create an economic revolution that will end a system that exploits most people for the good of a few.

Three: We must create a cultural revolution in the process, that will destroy the centuries of social programming we have undergone. It has been this programming that has made us see ourselves as inferior to men, that created the institution of marriage as a property relationship, that caused us to get little satisfaction from our work and leisure, that caused us to feel completely powerless and to accept that state of being.

The cultural aspect of the revolution has happened in very few other revolutions—usually the superstructure that developed under a previous economic system was maintained even after economic upheaval and reorganization. To prevent this from occurring in America, we must be organized before, during and after the initial struggles. We must all band together in Women's Liberation Groups, not as caucuses or auxiliaries of other organizations, but in our own organization that allows us to define our own goals and to determine our own programs. We must be active individually in other revolutionary organizations and take leadership roles in determining their programs, but each of us must be a part of a revolutionary woman's movement if real change in our condition is to occur.

What should we do?

Women in each class, in each culture (Black, Third World, Indian), will have to determine the most appropriate means of struggle for themselves. Revolutionary battles cannot begin until real wages are at least equal to those of men. Fight on those issues, and raise the questions we have outlined above about the kind of work we do and the conditions we live under. Don't wage union fights on *only* bread and butter issues.

Students and middle-class women have been meeting in small groups, no larger, usually, than twenty, to analyze the roots of their oppression as women. Such groups usually begin by focusing on people's immediate concerns, problems, and experiences, and then dig deeper by asking how those emerged . . . what institutions in society caused these conditions. What each participant once thought was her personal, individual problem, is in fact a social problem, shared by most in the group. It is a problem with institutional roots.

Secondly, the programming we each have undergone becomes clear. We can then build actions around the institutions that reinforce this programming—abortion laws, low wages, hiring discriminations, Bridal Fairs, Wall Street, Virginia Slims ads, etc.

We can build support services so that additional women can join with us. We should develop abortion funds and referral services, birth control information centers, child care facilities—all while pressuring appropriate institutions like the government and the work place to provide these services. This pressuring is not an end in itself; nor are the services we provide or the services the government and business may be forced to provide. Our goal is to raise consciousness by our own actions, and no action should be taken unless it is clear how that consciousness-raising process will be accomplished.

We must reach out and talk with other women. We can give courses on women's history at a local Free University, on campus, or in citywide forums. We can hold dorm meetings, workplace meetings, talk to women at trade and professional schools and prisons and try to develop new ways of communicating with each other (e.g., making films or "comic books").

We must act, as someone said at one of our conferences, as if the revolution had already begun. We must break through the Myth America image and create new ways of living and struggling with each other and with our brothers, as we destroy a system that will allow no growth of this kind. We must re-learn how to be human beings, and we must create the conditions so that others, too, can learn. *Viva la revolución.*

References

Baran, Paul and Paul Sweezy, *Monopoly Capital,* New York: Monthly Review Press, 1966.
Beard, Mary, *Woman as a Force in History,* New York: Macmillan Co., 1946.

Bird, Caroline, *Born Female,* New York: David McKay Co., Inc., 1968.
Engels, Friedrich, *Origins of the Family, Private Property and the State.*
Flexner, Eleanor, *A Century of Struggle,* Cambridge: Harvard University Press, 1959.
Friedan, Betty, *The Feminine Mystique,* New York: Dell, 1963.
Galbraith, John Kenneth, *The New Industrial State,* Boston: Houghton Mifflin Co., 1967.
Handbook on Women Workers, United States Dept. of Labor, Washington, D.C., 1965.
Jones, Beverly, *Towards a Female Liberation Movement,* part 1, Nashville: SSOC, 1968.
Komarovsky, Mirra, *Blue Collar Marriage,* New York: Random House, 1962.
Mills, C. Wright, *White Collar,* New York: Oxford University Press, 1951.
———————, *The Power Elite,* New York: Oxford University Press, 1965.
Packard, Vance, *The Hidden Persuaders,* New York: Pocket Books, Inc., 1957.
———————, *The Waste Makers,* New York: Pocket Books, Inc., 1960.
Rainwater, Lee, et al., *Workingman's Wife,* New York: MacFadden Books, 1959.
Sinclair, Andrew, *The Emancipation of American Women,* New York: Harper and Row, 1965.
Shofield, William, *Psychotherapy: The Purchase of Friendship,* New Jersey: Prentice Hall.
Veblen, Thorstein, *The Theory of the Leisure Class,* New York: Mentor, 1899.
Weber, Max, *The Protestant Ethic and the Spirit of Capitalism,* New York: Charles Scribner's Sons, 1958.
Wells, Lyn, *American Women: Their Use and Abuse,* Nashville: SSOC, 1969.

My House in the Trees
By Joan Joesting

And I sit by the window in my house in the trees
And think
And listen to the squirrels' social hour scattering leaves
Because it will not rain.
My mind rebels from my dissertation
To the window of the house in the trees
On the trafficless paved path road
To the house in the trees.

My dissertation is not on sex discrimination
But my house in the trees
Is what I love now that I can see the world with the leaves
gone
I want to write about the sickness of our society
And my trip to hell and back, only because I was born a female,
To get to my house in the trees.

I forget the cold Illinois winters and foundry summers doing
both man and woman's work on an unmechanized farm
And my marriage's legal prostitution
As I heal and grow
In my house in the trees.

I forget about the abortions that I could not get
And the beatings I could not get rid of
While running barefooted in the snow to call the sheriff
Who told me to solve my own marital problems
And "liberal" Illinois' male-made laws
Letting my husband take whatever he wished from our joint
checking account.

And then the mental prostitution
Of teaching in Illinois' "excellent" public schools
Listening to the white male principal tell me "You don't like to
do what
I say. You are bad, but you are a good teacher."

But then
I escaped to my house in the trees
And made the down payment with blood and those girl
babies who were lucky enough to be miscarried.
But today, I make my house payments with creativity and love
For my house in the trees
Where I heal all over and grow into a person, again
In my house in the trees.

WOODCUT: HOLY PROPOSAL
Marky Bulwinkle

♂ A Man's View

The fate of one sex is inseparable from that of the other, and any movement seeking to shatter one set of stereotypes must acknowledge the influence of the opposite stereotypes. So, it seems imperative that the prevailing assumptions about masculinity be exposed if we are to set free both the oppressors and the oppressed.

What are the prevailing myths about masculinity in our society? Masculinity seems to be synonymous with:

—rugged individualism.

—reason and utility as opposed to emotion and beauty, the latter being feminine, i.e. secondary.

—not showing emotion; being "cool" and ironic.

—not having to explain yourself to anyone or to take others' feelings into account.

—not making mistakes, or at least not admitting them.

—making the most difficult decisions almost automatically, without thinking twice and certainly without consulting anyone else.

—resolving conflicts through violence.

—commanding and then expecting to be obeyed, especially where women are concerned.

—taking what you want sexually when you want *it,* and disregarding *her.*

In short, masculinity means inherent superiority, hence autonomy, in all important matters. Weakness, doubt, discussion and compromise are signs of failure.

This James Bond concept of masculinity makes a lot of trouble for all of us. It fosters anxiety in men, since it is unattainable, and, where partially achieved, it is destructive rather than fulfilling. It is a direct insult to women, since it is based fundamentally on a doctrine of sexual supremacy. Indirectly, the fallacious view of masculinity makes women the targets of bitterness for men who hate and fear femininity in themselves—as hap-

By Andy Hawley ♂

pens to men who are raised by women, away from men, and yet are pressured to be masculine. Femininity in women becomes a necessary evil; in men it is evil, period. (This fear of being feminine, combined with the greater or lesser homoeroticism which is natural in all men, leads into an even stronger fear of being homosexual—which of course accelerates the whole vicious cycle of confusion, guilt, irritability and hostility.)

If everyone, women and men, could see that the whole business of sex identity is a red herring, then men could stop reinforcing all the wrong attitudes in each other through verbal cock-fighting, abusing women in front of other men, and ritual flirtation (the latter goes for women, too).

Our desire for social acceptance and our secret, lonely sense of being unable (as, luckily, most of us are) to live up to the male stereotype, have blinded us to the nature of our real needs and limits and our real opportunities for creating varied, happy lives. As American middle-class boys we were taught that our basic and ultimate motives are selfishly antisocial; moreover we, like our society, are confused and ambivalent about whether or not that's a good thing. In other words, we are a mixture of Puritan and hedonist. We are sheep who dream of being wolves, and who awake to feel self-hate at our secret wickedness and/or self-contempt at our timidity.

Thus women, for men, are alternately angels and slaves, to be worshipped one minute and spurned and exploited the next, but seldom treated as equals. Concerning sex, our society teaches total abstinence for the first decade of sexual maturity (even masturbation is considered at best unavoidable), then lifelong fidelity to one partner. All the while, society does its best both to keep us ignorant and confused about what a normal and well-developed sex life can be and to convince us that the forbidden fruits of promiscuity surpass anything the "moral" person will ever taste. What a bundle of paradoxes!

This last myth is possibly the cruelest joke of all. So ready are we to buy (literally) the notion that an evening in bed with the Playmate-of-the-Month is the greatest thing that could happen to us, that we ruthlessly suppress our real, protean, uncommercial fantasies and impulses, line the pockets of mountebanks like Hugh Hefner, and then congratulate ourselves on our liberal-mindedness! If instead we could face without flinching our homosexual impulses, our erotic feelings toward family, friends, strangers, our curiosity about how this or that act with such and such a person might feel—then we might be able to distinguish between an impulse, which is amoral and involuntary, and an action, which of course must be taken deliberately in accordance with its likely consequences and our overall values and goals.

What would happen if men rejected the male stereotype and acknowledged the value of openness, humility, discussion, consideration, cooperation, and compromise, along with honest, respectful disagreement and conflict?

We would trade our impossible standards and false self-image for realistic standards and real self-respect.

We would trade the dominance/submission syndrome for woman/man relationships that assume equality, honesty and good faith. We have to help each other become the kind of people we can love.

We would not deny the richness of our sexual imagination, nor the natural sexual element in all relationships. Just how it occurs—talking, touching, dancing, making love—should be our guilt-free choice, based on our own honest needs and values and our sensitivity to others, rather than a "moral" or "masculine" stereotype.

What about the question of "fidelity" to one partner versus a diverse sex life? Most adults need to have a primary relationship which comes before all others. If a problem in the primary relationship, which is the most demanding but also potentially the most rewarding kind, makes us try to escape through an outside flirtation or "affair," this is bad—not because of the sexual acts committed but because it *is* an escape. The problem remains unsolved.

Both gratification and consideration, both variety and responsibility, are important to us; and not only are they not mutually exclusive, they are interdependent. When we don't recognize the *equal* right of two people to gratification and consideration in sex and in general—and the great capacities we all have for getting pleasure from giving pleasure—then we withdraw into one of the myriad cop-outs available (such as cynical aloofness and Don Juan-ism).

As long as one is committed to the kind of "primary" relationship (usually marriage) mentioned above, its security and growth will outweigh all other considerations—which doesn't necessarily mean no experimentation or no sex outside the marriage.

All our relationships tend to be over-reserved; we need to loosen up and learn to express affection openly and physically. But the "primary" relationship—a deep, long-term commitment of a woman and a man to one another—is a unique, tremendously rich opportunity for self-knowledge, self-confidence, pleasure and generosity. In such a relationship, sex is both less and more than in a casual affair: less because only a part of the whole; more, because an expression and a consummation of the whole relationship.

These "changes of heart" are crucial. But change in consciousness must be accompanied (not preceded) by change in institutions.

Would men's and women's liberation of the sort I've described destroy or change the traditional American family? I think so. It is an institution with many drawbacks. While privacy and the sense that a spouse or child has of being special should not be valued lightly, considerations of efficiency and economy and of exposure to the difficulties and opportunities inherent in larger groups living and working together make it a good idea to experiment with some "communal" kinds of arrangement. Not only might it be possible to reduce the individual housework, cooking and child-care load, for examples, but some amount of group living affords intimate contact with a variety of people, multiple perspectives on oneself, and experience in dealing with group conflicts and decisions. This is a good way, especially for children, to break the cycle of selfish individualism and to move toward the sense of community that we need.

Whether or not we make such experiments, the following

changes in traditional family patterns seem to follow necessarily from liberated consciousness.

Women must be seriously involved in projects outside the home that are as challenging, broadening and socially consequential as any that men engage in. Whether or not this takes the form of a paying job is beside the point. But there is no reason why the woman's work might not be actually more remunerative than her husband's—the matter of financial support and the matter of socially useful work are not essentially related—at least, not in this society.

Men, by the same token, should take direct responsibility for a corresponding amount of the housekeeping chores. This is not a matter of rigid formulas; the point is that household chores need doing, there is no good reason the woman should have to do more of them than the man, and there are excellent reasons why she shouldn't. In the ideal society, of course, there may be women, just as there may be men, who really like housework and prefer to do it, but our goal is to establish a situation where men and women can approach this question without prejudice and with enough diverse experience and models to make an educated, individual choice.

The father should accept a more equal proportion of child-care responsibilities. This is even more important for the children than it is for the father and mother. Such an arrangement will help build good attitudes in the child about men's and women's roles, and will help eliminate the specialized "bedroom community" with its tired, estranged weekend fathers and its bored, resentful and slavishly ignorant housewife-mothers—hardly a good child-rearing environment.

Lastly—and here many will draw the line—women and men who accept the principle of equality must, if they are serious about it, become political agitators, constantly struggling to change *all* the institutions in their lives. Schools, business, church, family . . . all insult, exploit and oppress women. This system is so destructive of everyone it touches—and it touches everyone—that *it* must be destroyed. Oppression of women is so basic to our society that its destruction will constitute no less than a revolution.

Many draw the line at trying to change not only themselves but society. Considering the ridicule, hostility and resistance this women's struggle is encountering and will continue to encounter, that is understandable. But it is a vain hope. Personal liberation alone is impossible; escape is impossible. We need each other's support in taking the material and emotional risks involved in such struggles. Those risks can help give meaning and an air of reality to our relatively luxurious lives.

WOODCUT
Marky

♀———— **Witch Power**

W.I.T.C.H., otherwise known as the Women's International Terrorist Conspiracy from Hell, surfaced last Halloween. Their inaugural day began with an Up Against the Wall Street, all-day guerrilla theater procession in which the witches cast hexes on the Stock Exchange, declared "You Have a Fiend at Chase Manhattan" and created general terror and chaos. Halloween night the guerrilla witches flew through the Lower East Side, zapping all-male bars, girlie burlesque houses, and chic uptown-tourist infringements on the community.

WITCH is an all-woman Everything. It's theater, revolution, magic, terror, joy, garlic flowers, spells. It's an awareness that witches and gypsies were the original guerrilla and resistance fighters against oppression—particularly the oppression of women—down through the ages.

Witches have always been women who dared to be: groovy, courageous, aggressive, intelligent, non-conformist, explorative and curious, independent, sexually liberated, and revolutionary (this may explain why nine million women have been burned as witches).

Witches were the first friendly heads and dealers, the first birth-control practitioners and abortionists, the first alchemists (turn dross into gold and you devalue the whole idea of money!). They bowed to no man, being the living remnants of the oldest culture of all—one in which men and women were equal sharers in a truly cooperative society, before the death-dealing sexual, economic, and spiritual repression of the "Imperialist Phallic Society" took over and began to shit all over nature and human life.

A witch lives and laughs in every woman. She is the free part of each of us, beneath the shy smiles, the acquiescence to absurd male domination, the makeup or flesh-suffocating clothing our sick society demands. There is no "joining" WITCH.

By W.I.T.C.H. ♀

If you are a woman, and dare to look within yourself, you are a witch. You make your own rules. You are free and beautiful. You can be invisible or evident in how you choose to make your witch-self known.

You can form your own Coven of sister witches, do your own actions. Whatever is repressive, solely male-oriented, greedy, puritanical, authoritarian—those are your targets. Your weapons are theater, magic, satire, explosions, herbs, music, costumes, masks, chants, stickers, stencils and paint, bricks, brooms, guns, voodoo dolls, cats, candles, bells, chalk, your own boundless beautiful imagination. Your power comes from your own self as a woman, and from sharing, rapping, and acting in concert with your sisters. You are pledged to free our brothers from oppression and stereotyped sexual roles, as well as ourselves.

You are a witch by being female, untamed, angry, joyous and immortal. You are a witch by saying aloud, "I am a witch" and thinking about that.

WOODCUT:
FETISH
Marky

WOODCUT:
QUEEN
Marky

♀ Kinder, Küche, Kirche as Scientific Law: Psychology Constructs the Female

Psychologists have set about describing the true nature of women with an enthusiasm and absolute certainty which is rather disquieting. Bruno Bettelheim, of the University of Chicago, tells us (1965) that "we must start with the realization that, as much as women want to be good scientists or engineers, they want first and foremost to be womanly companions of men and to be mothers."

Erik Erikson of Harvard University (1964), upon noting that young women often ask whether they can "have an identity before they know whom they will marry, and for whom they will make a home," explains somewhat elegiacally that "much of a young woman's identity is already defined in her kind of attractiveness and in the selectivity of her search for the man (or men) by whom she wishes to be sought. . . ." Mature womanly fulfillment, for Erikson, rests on the fact that a woman's ". . . somatic design harbors an 'inner space' destined to bear the offspring of chosen men, and with it, a biological, psychological, and ethical commitment to take care of human infancy."

Some psychiatrists even see the acceptance of woman's role by women as a solution to societal problems. "Woman is nurturance . . . ," writes Joseph Rheingold (1964), a psychiatrist at Harvard Medical School; ". . . anatomy decrees the life of a woman . . . when women grow up without dread of their biological functions and without subversion by feminist doctrine, and therefore enter upon motherhood with a sense of fulfillment and altruistic sentiment, we shall attain the goal of a good life and a secure world in which to live it."

These views from men of high prestige reflect a fairly general consensus: liberation for women will consist first in their attractiveness, so that second, they may obtain the kinds of homes (and men) which will allow joyful altruism and nurturance.

Business does not disagree. If views such as Bettelheim's and Erikson's do indeed have something to do with real liberation

By Naomi Weisstein 

for women, then seldom in human history has so much money and effort been spent on helping a group of people realize their true potential. Clothing, cosmetics and home furnishings are multi-million dollar businesses: if you don't like investing in firms that make weaponry and flaming gasoline, there's a lot of cash in "inner space."

It is an interesting but limited exercise to show that psychologist's ideas of women's nature fit so remarkably the common prejudice and serve industry and commerce so well. Just because it's good for business doesn't mean it's wrong. *It is wrong,* and there isn't the tiniest shred of evidence that these fantasies of servitude and childish dependence have anything to do with women's true potential. The idea of the nature of human possibility which rests on the accidents of individual development or genitalia, on what is possible today because of what happened yesterday, on the fundamentalist myth of sex organ causality, has strangled and deflected psychology so that it is relatively useless in describing, explaining, or predicting humans and their behavior. Present psychology is less than worthless in contributing to a vision which could truly liberate—men as well as women.

Psychology has nothing to say about what women are really like, what they need and what they want, essentially, because psychology does not know. This failure is not limited to women; rather, the kind of psychology which has addressed itself to how people act and who they are has failed to understand, in the first place, why people act the way they do, and has certainly failed to understand what might make them act differently.

The kind of psychology which has addressed itself to these questions is in large part clinical psychology and psychiatry, which in America means endless commentary and refinement of Freudian theory. Here, the causes of failure are obvious and appalling: Freudians and neo-Freudians, and clinicians and psychiatrists in general, have simply refused to look at the evidence against their theory and their practice, and have used as evidence for their theory and their practice stuff so flimsy and transparently biased as to have absolutely no standing as empirical evidence. But even psychology which conforms to rigorous methodology has gone about looking at people in such a way as to have limited usefulness. This is because it has been a central assumption for most psychologists of human personality that human behavior rests primarily on an individual and inner dynamic, perhaps fixed in infancy, perhaps fixed by genitalia, perhaps simply arranged in a rather immovable cognitive network.

This assumption is rapidly losing ground as personality psychologists fail again and again to get consistency in the assumed personalities of their subjects (Block, 1968) and as the evidence collects that what a person does and who he believes himself to be will in general be a function of what people around him expect him to be, and what the overall situation in which he is acting implies that he is. Compared to the influence of the social context within which a person lives, his or her history and "traits," as well as biological makeup, may simply be random variations, "noise" superimposed on the true signal which can predict behavior.

To summarize: the first reason for psychology's failure to understand what people are and how they act is that clinicians and psychiatrists, who are generally the theoreticians on these matters, have essentially made up myths without any evidence to support these myths. The second reason for psychology's failure is that personality theory has looked for inner traits when it should have been looking at social context.

The first cause of failure is the acceptance by psychiatrists and clinical psychologists of theory without evidence. If we inspect the literature of personality, it is immediately obvious that the bulk of it is written by clinicians and psychiatrists, and that the major support for their theories is "years of intensive clinical experience." This is a tradition started by Freud. His "insights" occurred during the course of his work with his patients. There is nothing wrong with such an approach to theory *formulation;* a person is free to make up theories with any inspiration which works: divine revelation, intensive clinical practice, a random number table. But he is not free to claim any validity for his theory until it has been tested and confirmed.

Theories are treated in no such tentative way in ordinary clinical practice. Consider Freud. What he thought constituted evidence violated the most minimal conditions of scientific rigor. In *The Sexual Enlightenment of Children,* the classic document which is supposed to demonstrate empirically the existence of a castration complex and its connection to a phobia, Freud based his analysis on the reports of the father of the little boy, himself in therapy, and a devotee of Freudian theory. I really don't have to comment further on the contamination in this kind of evidence. It is remarkable that only recently Freud's classic theory on the sexuality of women—the notion of the double orgasm—has been tested physiologically and found plain wrong.

Those who claim that fifty years of psychoanalytic experience constitute evidence enough of the essential truths of Freud's theory should ponder the robust health of the double orgasm. Did women, until Masters and Johnson (1966), believe they were having two different kinds of orgasm? Did their psychiatrists cow them into reporting something that was not true? If so, were there other things they reported that were also not true? Did psychiatrists ever learn anything different from what their theories had led them to believe? If clinical experience means anything at all, surely we should have been done with the double orgasm myth long before the Masters and Johnson studies.

But certainly, you may object, "years of intensive clinical experience" is the only reliable measure in a discipline which rests for its findings on insight, sensitivity, and intuition. The problem with insight, sensitivity, and intuition is that these can confirm for all time the biases that one started out with. People used to be absolutely convinced of their ability to tell which of their number were engaging in witchcraft.

Years of intensive clinical experience is not the same thing as empirical evidence. The first thing an experimenter learns in any kind of experiment which involves humans is the concept of the "double blind." The term is taken from medical experiments, where one group is given a drug which is presumably supposed to change behavior in a certain way, and a control group is given a placebo. If the observers or the subjects know which group took which drug, the result invariably comes out on the positive side for the new drug. Only when it is not known which subject took which pill is validity remotely approximated.

In judgments of human behavior, it is so difficult to precisely tie down just what behavior is going on, let alone what behavior should be expected, that one must test again and again the reliability of judgments. How many judges, blind, will agree in their observations? Can they replicate their own judgments at some later time? When, in actual practice, these judgment criteria are tested for clinical judgments, then we find that the judges cannot judge reliably nor can they judge consistently: they do no better than chance in identifying which of a certain set of stories were written by men and which by women; which of a whole battery of clinical test results are the products of homosexuals and which are the products of heterosexuals (Hooker, 1957) and which, of a battery of clinical test results *and* interviews (where questions are asked such as "do you have delusions" and "what are your symptoms?") (Little & Schneidman, 1959), are products of psychotics, neurotics, psychosomatics, or normals.

Lest this summary escape your notice, let me stress the implications of these findings. The ability of judges, chosen for their clinical expertise, to distinguish male heterosexuals from male homosexuals on the basis of three widely used clinical projective tests—the Rorschach, the TAT, and the MAP, was *no better than chance*. The reason this is such devastating news, of course, is that sexuality is considered by personality theorists to be of fundamental importance in the deep dynamic of personality; if what is considered gross sexual deviance cannot be caught, then what are psychologists talking about when they claim, for instance, that at the basis of paranoid psychosis is "latent homosexual panic"? They can't even identify what homosexual anything is, let alone "latent homosexual panic"!

More frightening, expert clinicians cannot be consistent on what diagnostic category to assign to a person, again on the basis of both tests and interviews; a number of normals in the

Little & Schneidman study were described as psychotic, in such categories as "schizophrenic with homosexual tendencies," or "schizoid character with depressive trends." But most disheartening, when the judges were asked to rejudge the test protocols some weeks later, their diagnosis of the same subjects on the basis of the same protocol differed markedly from their initial judgments. It is obvious that even simple descriptive conventions in clinical psychology cannot be consistently applied; that these descriptive conventions have any explanatory significance is therefore, of course, out of the question.

As a student in a graduate class at Harvard, some years ago, I was a member of a seminar which was asked to identify which of two piles of a clinical test, the TAT, had been written by males, and which of the two piles had been written by females. Only four students out of twenty identified the piles correctly, and this was after one and a half months of intensively studying the differences between men and women. Since this result is below chance, that is, this result would occur by chance about four out of a thousand times, we may conclude that there *is* finally a consistency here; students are judging knowledgeably within the context of psychological teaching about the differences between men and women; the teachings themselves are erroneous.

Ah, you may argue, the theory may be scientifically "unsound" but at least it cures people. There is no evidence that it does. In 1952, Eysenck reported the results of what is called an "outcome of therapy" study of neurotics which showed that, of the patients who received psychoanalysis, the improvement rate was 44%; of the patients who received psychotherapy, the improvement rate was 64%; and the patients who received no treatment at all, the improvement rate was 72%. These findings have never been refuted; subsequent later studies have confirmed the negative results of the Eysenck study. (Barron and Leary, 1955; Bergin, 1963; Cartwright and Vogel, 1960; Truax, 1963)

How can clinicians and psychiatrists then, in all good conscience, continue to practice? Largely by ignoring these results and being careful not to do outcome-of-therapy studies. The attitude is nicely summarized by Rotter (1960) (quoted in Astin, 1961): "Research studies in psychotherapy tend to be concerned more with some aspects of the psychotherapeutic procedure and less with outcome . . . to some extent, it reflects an interest in the psychotherapy situation as a kind of personality laboratory." Some laboratory.

Thus, we can conclude that since clinical experience and tools can be shown to be worse than useless when tested for consistency, efficacy, agreement, and reliability, we can safely conclude that theories of a clinical nature advanced about women are also worse than useless. It has become increasingly clear that in order to understand why people do what they do, and certainly in order to change what people do, psychologists must turn away from the theory of the causal nature of the inner dynamic and look to the social context within which individuals live.

Block's work (1968) established that personality tests never yield consistent predictions; a rigid authoritarian on one measure will be unauthoritarian on the next. But the reason for this inconsistency is only now becoming clear, and it seems overwhelmingly to have much more to do with the social situation in which the subject finds himself than with the subject himself.

In a series of brilliant experiments, Rosenthal and his coworkers (Rosenthal and Jacobson, 1968; Rosenthal, 1966) have shown that if one group of experimenters has one hypothesis about what they expect to find, and another group of experimenters has the opposite hypothesis, both groups will obtain results in accord with their hypotheses. Thus, in a success rating task, where subjects were required to rate faces cut out from magazines on a twenty-point scale from −10, very unsuccessful, to +10, highly successful, the group of subjects whose experimenters had been told would rate the faces high, had mean ratings, in every case, above the highest mean rating for the group of subjects whose experimenters expected the subjects to rate the faces low.

In all, about 375 subjects were tested; the results would have happened by chance about one in one thousand times. The experimenters were instructed to read the same set of instructions, and to say no more than was in the instructions; obviously, the cues which influenced subjects were nonverbal. Even with animals, in two separate studies (Rosenthal & Fode, 1960; Rosenthal & Lawson, 1961), those experimenters who were told that rats learning mazes had been especially bred for brightness obtained better learning from their rats than did experimenters believing their rats to have been bred for dullness. These results would have happened by chance one out of one hundred times.

In a very recent study, Rosenthal & Jacobson (1968) extended their analysis to the natural classroom situation. Here, they found that when teachers expected randomly selected students to "show great promise," these students' I.Q.'s increased significantly from control group students, with the most dramatic increments in the area of reasoning ability.

Thus, even in carefully controlled experiments, and with no outward or conscious difference in behavior, the hypotheses we start with will influence enormously the behavior of another organism. These studies are extremely important when assessing the validity of psychological studies of women. Since it is fairly safe to say that most of us start with hypotheses as to the nature of men and women, the validity of a number of observations of sex differences is questionable, even when these observations have been taken under carefully controlled conditions.

Second, and more importantly, the Rosenthal experiments point quite clearly to the influence of social expectation. In some extremely important ways, people are what you expect them to be or at least they behave as you expect them to behave. Thus, if women, according to Bruno Bettelheim, want first and foremost to be good wives and mothers, it is extremely likely that that is what Bettelheim, and the rest of the society, want them to be.

There is another series of social psychological experiments which points to the inescapable overwhelming effect of social context in an extremely vivid way. These are the obedience experiments of Stanley Milgram (1965), concerned with the extent to which subjects in psychological experiments will obey the orders of unknown experimenters, even when these orders carry them to the distinct possibility that the subject is killing somebody.

Briefly, a subject is made to administer electric shocks in ascending 15-volt increments to another person whom the subject believes to be another subject, but who is in fact a stooge. The voltages range from 15 to 450 volts; for each four consecutive voltages there are verbal descriptions such as "mild shock," "danger, severe shock," and finally, for the 435- and 450-volt switches, simply a red XXX marked over the switches. The stooge, as the voltage increases, begins to cry out against the pain; he then screams that he has a heart condition, begging the subject to stop, and finally, he goes limp and stops responding altogether at a certain voltage. Since even at this point, the subject is instructed to keep increasing the voltage, it is possible for the subjects to continue all the way up to the end switch—450 volts.

The percentage of subjects who do so is quite high; all in all, about one thousand subjects were run, and about sixty-five percent would go to the end switch in an average experiment. No tested individual differences between subjects predicted which of the subjects would continue to obey, and which would break off the experiment. Predictions were far below actual percentages, with an average prediction that three percent of the subjects would obey to the end. But, even though psychiatrists have no idea of how people are going to behave in this situation (despite one of the central facts of the twentieth century, which is that people have been made to kill enormous numbers of other people), and even though individual differences do not predict which subjects are going to obey and which are not, it is very easy to predict when subjects will be obedient and when they will be defiant. All the experimenter has to do is change the social situation. In a variant of the experiment (Milgram, 1965), when two other stooges who were also administering electric shocks refused to continue, only ten percent of the subjects continued to the end switch. This is critical for personality theory, for it indicates that the lawful behavior is the behavior that can be predicted from the social situation, not from the individual history.

Finally, an ingenious experiment by Schachter and Singer (1962) showed that subjects injected with adrenalin, which produces a state of physiological arousal in all but minor respects identical to that which occurs when subjects are extremely afraid, became euphoric when they were in a room with a stooge who was acting euphoric, and became extremely angry when they were placed in a room with a stooge who was acting extremely angry.

To summarize: if subjects under quite innocuous and noncoercive social conditions can be made to kill other subjects and under other types of social conditions will positively refuse to do so; if subjects can react to a state of physiological fear by becoming euphoric because there is somebody else euphoric, if students become intelligent because teachers expect them to be intelligent, and rats run mazes better because experimenters are told that the rats are bright, then it is obvious that a study of human behavior requires, first and foremost, a study of the social contexts within which people move, the expectations as to how they will behave, and the authority which tells them who they are and what they are supposed to do.

Two theories of the nature of women, which come not from psychiatric and clinical tradition but from biology, can be disposed of with little difficulty. The first argument notices social interaction in primate groups, and observes that females are submissive and passive. Putting aside for a moment the serious problem of experimenter bias (for instance, Harlow (1962) of the University of Wisconsin, after observing differences between male and female rhesus monkeys, quotes Lawrence Sterne to the effect that women are silly and trivial, and concludes that "men and women have differed in the past and they will differ in the future"), the problem with the argument from primate groups is that the crucial experiment has not been performed. The crucial experiment would manipulate or change the social organization of these groups, and watch the subsequent behavior. Until then, we must conclude that, since primates are, at present, too stupid to change their social conditions by themselves, the "innateness" and fixedness of their behavior is simply not known. As applied to humans, the argument becomes patently irrelevant, since the most salient feature of human social organization is its variety; and there are a number of cultures where there is at least a rough equality between men and women (Mead, 1949). Thus, primate arguments tell us little.

The second theory of sex differences argues that since females and males differ in their sex hormones and sex hormones enter the brain (Hamburg and Lunde in Maccoby, 1966), there must be innate differences in "nature." But the only thing this argument tells us is that there are differences in the physiological state. The problem is whether these differences are at all relevant to behavior. Recall that Schachter and Singer (1962) have shown that a particular physiological state can itself lead to a multiplicity of felt emotional states and outward behavior, depending on the social situation.

In brief, the uselessness of present psychology with regard to women is simply a special case of the general conclusion: one must understand social expectations about women if one is going to characterize the behavior of women.

How are women characterized in our culture, and in psychology? They are inconsistent, emotionally unstable, lacking in a strong conscience or super-ego, weaker, "nurturant" rather than productive, "intuitive" rather than intelligent, and, if they are at all "normal," suited to the home and the family. In short, the list adds up to a typical minority group stereotype of inferiority (Hacker, 1951): if they know their place, which is in the home, they are really quite lovable, happy, childlike, loving creatures.

In a review of the intellectual differences between little boys and little girls, Eleanor Maccoby (1966) has shown that there are no intellectual differences until about high school, or, if there are, girls are slightly ahead of boys. At high school, girls begin to do worse on a few intellectual tasks, such as arithmetical reasoning, and beyond high school, the achievement of women now measured in terms of accomplishment drops off even more rapidly.

There are a number of other, non-intellectual tests which show sex differences: I choose the intellectual differences since it is seen clearly that women start becoming inferior. It is no use to talk about women being different but equal; all of the tests I can think of have a "good" outcome and a "bad" outcome. Women usually end up at the "bad" outcome. In light of social expectations about women, what is surprising is not that women end up where society expects they will; what is surprising is that little girls don't get the message that they are supposed to be stupid until high school; and what is even more remarkable is that some women resist this message even after high school, college, and graduate school.

I began with remarks on the task of discovering the limits of human potential. Until psychologists realize that it is they who are limiting discovery of human potential by their refusal to accept evidence, if they are clinical psychologists, or, if they are rigorous, by their assumption that people move in a context-free ether with only their innate dispositions and their individual traits determining what they will do, then psychology will have nothing of substance to offer in this task. I don't know what immutable differences exist between men and women apart from differences in their genitals; perhaps there are some other unchangeable differences; probably there are a number of irrelevant differences. But it is clear that until social expectations for men and women are equal, until we provide equal respect for both men and women, our answers to this question will simply reflect our prejudices.

References

Astin, A. W. The functional autonomy of psychotherapy. *American Psychologist,* 1961, *16,* 75-78.

Barron, F. & Leary, T. Changes in psychoneurotic patients with and without psychotherapy. *Journal of Consulting Psychology,* 1955, *19,* 239-245.

Bergin, A. E. The effects of psychotherapy: negative results revisited. *Journal of Counseling Psychology,* 1963, *10,* 244-250.

Bettelheim, B. The commitment required of a woman entering a scientific profession in present day American society. *Woman and the Scientific Professions,* The M.I.T. symposium on American Women in Science and Engineering, 1965.

Block, J. Some reasons for the apparent inconsistency of personality. *Psychological Bulletin,* 1968, *70,* 210-212.

Cartwright, R. D. & Vogel, J. L. A comparison of changes in psychoneurotic patients during matched periods of therapy and no-therapy. *Journal of Consulting Psychology,* 1960, *24,* 121-127.

Erikson, E. Inner and outer space: reflections on womanhood. *Daedalus,* 1964, *93,* 582-606.

Eysenck, H. J. The effects of psychotherapy: an evaluation. *Journal of Consulting Psychology,* 1952, *16,* 319-324.

Fieldcrest—Advertisement in the *New York,* 1965.

Freud, S. *The Sexual Enlightenment of Children,* Collier Books Edition, 1963.

Goldstein, A. P. & Dean, S. J. *The Investigation of Psychotherapy: Commentaries and Readings.* John Wiley & Sons, New York: 1966.

Hamburg, D. A. & Lunde, D. T. Sex hormones in the development of sex differences in human behavior. In Maccoby, Ed. *The Development of Sex Differences,* 1-24, Stanford University Press, 1966.

Hacker, H. M. Women as a minority group. *Social Forces,* 1951, *30,* 60-69.

Harlow, H. F. The heterosexual affectional system in monkeys. *The American Psychologist,* 1962, *17,* 1-9.

Hooker, E. Male Homosexuality in the Rorschach. *Journal of Projective Techniques,* 1957, *21,* 18-31.

Little, K. B. & Schneidman, E. S. Congruences among interpretations of psychological test and anamnestic data. *Psychological Monographs,* 1959, *73,* 1-42.

Maccoby, Eleanor E. Sex differences in intellectual functioning, in Maccoby, Ed. *The Development of Sex Differences,* 25-55. Stanford University Press, 1966.

Masters, W. H. & Johnson, V. E. *Human Sexual Response,* Little, Brown: Boston, 1966.

Mead, M. *Male and Female: a study of the sexes in a changing world,* William Morrow, New York, 1949.

Milgram, S. Some Conditions of Obedience and Disobedience to Authority. *Human Relations,* 18, 1965a, 57-76.

Milgram, S. Liberating effects of group pressure. *Journal of Personality and Social Psychology,* 1, 1965b, 127-134.

Powers, E. & Witmer, H. *An experiment in the prevention of delinquency,* New York: Columbia University Press, 1951.

Rheingold, J. *The fear of being a woman.* Grune & Stratton, New York: 1964.

Rosenthal, R. On the social psychology of the psychological experiment: The experimenter's hypothesis as unintended determinant of experimental results. *American Scientist,* 1963, 51, 286-283.

Rosenthal, R. *Experimenter Effects in Behavioral Research.* New York: Appleton-Century-Crofts, 1966.

Rosenthal, R. & Jacobson, L. *Pygmalion in the classroom: teacher expectation and pupils' intellectual development.* New York: Holt, Rinehart & Winston, 1968.

Rosenthal, R. & Lawson, R. A longitudinal study of the effects of experimenter bias on the operant learning of laboratory rats. Unpublished manuscript, Harvard University, 1961.

Rosenthal, R. & Fode, K. L. The effect of experimenter bias on the performance of the albino rat. Unpublished manuscript, Harvard University, 1960.

Rotter, J. B. Psychotherapy. *Annual Review of Psychology,* 1960, *11,* 381-414.

Schachter, S. & Singer, J. E. Cognitive, social, and psychological determinants of emotional state. *Psychological Review,* 1962, *69,* 379-399.

Truax, C. B. Effective ingredients in psychotherapy: an approach to unraveling the patient-therapist interaction. *Journal of Counseling Psychology,* 1963, *10,* 256-263.

♀ About a month ago we were given, by chance, the March-April issue of *motive* on Women's Liberation. We immediately recognized it as the most creative gathering together of intelligent views on the subject that we have seen.

We ordered additional copies for our members who all reacted with enthusiasm and praise. We felt strongly that the content and format combined with great impact and that this issue of *motive* should be required reading for all American women and men.

We read with dismay in the *New York Times* "an especially intense controversy arose over the March-April issue . . . in which a number of four-letter words were used." We were greatly concerned to read further that this controversy prompted Dr. Myron F. Wicke to consider censorship of the magazine.

Dr. Wicke, in stating that "there is enough obscenity in the world without our adding to it," seems to be confusing the literary use of "common" vocabulary with the true obscenities of universal inhumanity and selfish hatred. The pursuit of true Christian morality in the modern world is of prime importance. With the world in its present state of chaos, such arguments about vocabulary are trivial and time-wasting. The words which presumably offended Dr. Wicke are in any case, as you pointed out in your editorial, *part* of the subject. Putting one's head in the sand will not make the problem go away.

Your March-April issue gave us both the professional's assessment and the artist's perception of woman's situation. This unique combination should definitely be republished in book form.

National Organization for Women
Central New Jersey Chapter

Letters

☐
☐ Stop sending this Garbage to the students in our Colleges. Good for outhouses in the mountain country.

A Tax Payer and Loyal American

♂ As most "red-blooded" American males I should respond to the March-April issue of *motive* with resentment and indignation. However, good sense does on an occasion win over the emotion of male pride, and superior journalism deserves to be recognized. So, I wish to be among those "old men" who commend *motive* for its excellence in publishing the "female issue" of March-April.

I assume that many letters have come to your desk condemning the content of the issue, and perhaps more vehemently, some of the language. I trust however that those in responsible positions of leadership, such as those on the *motive* editorial board, are quick enough to distinguish between profanity and the language of the real world. Surely the most profane and demeaning phrase of our time when speaking of women is "her place is in the kitchen," which, compared to "bitch" and like words, is far more scurrilous.

Thank the girls for a job well done, and I continue to look forward to each issue as usual.

East Lansing, Michigan

♂ Your latest hot issue on the Freed Woman might lead some unsuspecting young women astray (as happened to Miss Cooke at the conference for women's rights). It's a hell of a world when a woman is made to feel guilty about enjoying the role of housewife, homemaker, and mother! True, there are women who are happier out working. Let them have equal rights and equal pay because they work just as hard as do men—this is something to fight for. But for some lucky women, fulfillment can be found at home doing the same kinds of things Grandma did—making the home the center of warmth, love and nurture.

In this crazy world of computers, wars, and crass commercialism, it is up to the women to put human values first. It is the wife's job to meet her husband morning and evening, to share some things in common, and to provide beauty and comfort in herself and in the home. It is the job of the mother to be home when her children are there—not as a slave to their needs—but as someone who cares and has time to listen, one who can help them grow up with understanding and love. If Mrs. works at being woman of the world all day, her life is aimed for the job, the others, the self outside the home. She rushes out early, giving everyone in the family a do-it-yourself job. When she comes home after a day in the world outside—unlike Mr. who can relax from his job—she goes into high gear to tackle the T.V. dinners and household requirements. Unless they both take on the home chores, something has to give—what?

Time for relationships, time to listen, time to make a real pie. It is no coincidence that the divorce and delinquency rates are directly proportional to the freedom of the "liberated" working wife. The home becomes only a clearing house for busy people—all going their own way. The family as we know it becomes obsolete. Satisfying human relationships have to be sought elsewhere. I am not advocating that women just stay home to slave and serve. In this day of housework convenience, a woman has time to develop herself as an individual and it is essential that she does this. It is a wise woman who educates herself and her daughters for a specific vocation, not only for her own self realization but for the necessity or desire to work at some stage in her life when it can be conveniently fitted into the family schedule. It is an even wiser woman who realizes that her role in the home is the first and most important job—the cultivating of human relationships in an atmosphere of love.

Dynnyrne, Hobart
Tasmania

♀ My heartfelt congratulations to you for your special double issue on THE LIBERATION OF WOMEN! I have always considered *motive* the best of the myriad of magazines to which my husband and I subscribe, and both of us are grateful for this particular issue.

In particular let me commend you on "Here's to You, Mrs. Robinson," with its paragraph in defense of the four-letter words which are used in other articles. It made me realize how ridiculously I have allowed myself to continue to be shocked by them, without going the next step—namely of demythologizing them. Of course it's the concepts that make them bad. Thanks for pointing this out so well.

All the articles are extremely well written and to the point about the conflicts which most of us have had for so long, but have been unable to articulate as well and as publicly so that they can be discussed seriously—hopefully with the intent of resolution.

Again—countless thanks for an outstanding issue!

Bronx, New York

The Pill—Radio News 2/24/70
By Marilyn Lowen Fletcher

10–15% of women on The Pill have decreased
desire and pleasure in sex

a small % report increased (what they call) "sexual
pleasure"

Psychological effects of the pill were reported to be:
morbidity
depression
sleep disturbances (too much or not enough)
feelings of inferiority

This is true   Scientifically documented by
scientific impartial research.
Now I know what was wrong with me all that
time I was taking the pill and wondering
what was wrong with me/why can't i pull
myself together.

> Slow Death—while waiting for
> cervical cancer or blood clots
> and hoping to avoid death by
> some butcher abortionist

PHOTOGRAPH
Martin S. Dworkin

♀

You've Come A Long Way, Baby —Women in the Movement

The treatment of women in the movement reflects the treatment of women in the dominant society. That testimony sums up the experiences of most of the movement women I've known in recent years.

As women we accuse men in North American society of being domineering, aggressive and competitive. Men treat women as sex objects and make them the drudge workers; men do not listen to women or think women have brains. These patterns are apparent in prevailing American society, but they also describe the movement.

There is a popular movement saying which claims, "She is just joining the movement because she's in love with him (some big shot leader in the movement)." This myth has been exploded in various informal surveys taken among radical women. Although the charge is occasionally accurate, it ignores the larger and more fundamental truth that most women get involved in radical political movements because of an awareness (often unconscious) of their own oppression.

"The only position for women in SNCC is prone."

—STOKELY CARMICHAEL, OCT., 1964

This aptly expresses the Student Nonviolent Coordinating Committee's attitude toward women in general; the attitude toward white women was even worse. White women were not permitted to do voter registration work, but were relegated to teaching and community center work with old people and little kids. White women were not permitted to leave their homes after dark. Use of project funds or cars was forbidden and, of course, women were expected to do the laundry, cooking and cleaning. The first question when a woman arrived at a project was "Can you type?" The first paid SNCC worker was Jane Stembridge, who was the typist. Jane later proved to be a very gifted poet.

By Linda Seese

The hierarchy of SNCC was black man, black woman, white man and then white woman. White women often felt that they were fighting for the equality of black men at the expense of their own. Such policies were rationalized on the basis of possible adverse reactions by the local whites and a desire not to reinforce the matriarchal societal and familial structure of poor blacks (it seems that some SNCC people and Moynihan had something in common).

Despite these restrictions, some women achieved the freedom to organize and did a fine job of it. Because it was obvious that no white woman could gain a power position in SNCC, none tried; they were therefore free to organize in their communities. The cotton pickers' strike and the Mississippi Freedom Labor Union (MFLU) arose in a town which had had one white woman as its only organizer for ten months.

White women saw the black matriarchal society and began to discover an alternative to the lives of their white, middle-class mothers. We realized the biological-inferiority-of-women argument to be a lie and a myth. We saw women manage jobs and families. We saw women rule their own roosts, not merely deciding what color car to buy. We noted that the leadership of the Southern grassroots organizations—MFLU and Mississippi Freedom Democratic Party (MFDP)—was female. We met Fannie Lou Hamer, a truly great person, who is also a *woman*. At the same time, we saw the dangers of the matriarchal society—the oppression of black men. We do not advocate such a society; we do wonder why people condone the oppression of all women everywhere while they condemn the oppression of black men.

Simultaneous with these Southern experiences, there were women in Students for a Democratic Society (SDS) and its community organizing branch, ERAP, who were working very hard to build a radical movement. They were doing an excellent job, in part because women seemed better able to endure the monotonies that became commonplace after the excitement had worn off. Women seemed better able to relate to people and less inclined to engage in "ego trips." (Both of these advantages were probably due to early training and expectations and it is a shame that men were not trained for some of the same talents.) These women, however, faced the same restrictions as their sisters in the South, though the insults were less blatant. On many ERAP projects, one or two men held so much power that there was no room for anyone else—male or female. On some projects, attempts to organize women on women's issues were stopped by male project members. Occasionally, men shared the domestic chores of the project, and in Cleveland, women led the white community organizing project. But these were the exceptions, achieved by a few women after much struggle and many insults. Women who struggled for even such tidbits of equality were not "real women," said some movement men.

Gradually, it became apparent that there are two roles for women in the movement—workers and wives:

> One role for women is servicing the organization's men. These women maintain the stable, homey atmosphere which the radical male needs to survive. They raise the future radicals of Canada. They earn the money in the mundane jobs that our society pays people to do, so the radical men can be at home and be political and creative. . . . But in order to do this, these men need followers and maintainers. Thus, the workers of the movement—the typists, fund-raisers and community organizers.[1]

Some SDS women recognized their position in a slightly different way:

> The movement for social change taught women activists about their own oppression. Politically, women were excluded from decision-making. They typed, made leaflets, did the shit-work. The few women who attained leadership positions had to struggle against strong convention.
>
> Also, women in the movement were in a unique situation. As some got married, they found that there were no models for a marriage

[1] Bernstein, Morton, Seese and Wood, "Sisters, Brothers, Lovers . . . Listen," published by New Left Committee, Toronto, 1967.

in which both man and woman were politically active. Was the once active woman now to assume a supportive role, to stay home with the kids or get an unwanted job to support her activist husband? Were both partners' interests to have equal weight in determining what kind of work they would do, where they would live?[2]

Other aspects of the oppression of women in the movement were the loss of many members—women left in droves—and the failure to recruit many others who were turned off by the hypocrisy that permitted women to remain in servile positions, that refused to listen to women in meetings, and that even dared to deny that women were oppressed. We have had to face the fact that many of our talented sisters became so demoralized and hurt by their treatment in the movement that they are gone. The movement had closed all channels to one-half of its membership.

Another phenomenon of this oppression was the movement bitch. Women who wanted to assert themselves often had to scream and rage to be listened to. So, they were labeled bitches and few men ever wondered how they got that way. Other women who rose to positions of some power were no longer seen as women. To be equal to a man meant to lose all attractiveness.

The Women's Liberation Movement grew rapidly from a few isolated women seeking justice, to Feminine Caucuses within the movement, to the formation of separate women's liberation groups.

During the community organizing period—approximately 1963–1966—women fought against their oppression as they have always done, on a one-to-one basis in their personal relations or to gain some measure of power in the local project. Most women felt this kind of struggle was enough. Their lack of strength on an organizational level was not important, because they were not interested in being big shots, anyway.

[2] Booth, Goldfield, and Munaker, "Toward a Radical Movement," *Voice of Women's Liberation Movement* Newsletter, April 1968.

A few rare women realized their oppression and that it was hurting women—stifling their potential—and hurting the movement. The first woman to raise the cry of dissent was Ruby Doris Smith Robinson, a young black who was the chief administrator for SNCC—in charge of personnel, cars and finances. Ruby Doris, a founding member of SNCC, was a tough, strong woman with a large heart. It was her paper, *The Position of Women in SNCC,* presented at a conference in October 1964 which evoked Stokely's famous remark quoted above. The response, of course, was laughter and there was no discussion of the paper. This—to the most powerful woman in SNCC!

In the fall of 1965, Casey Hayden and Mary King, two white women from the South who had been very active in SNCC and ERAP for years, wrote an article on women in the movement in the now-defunct journal, *Studies on the Left.* A year later, Heather Dean, a staff member of the Student Union for Peace Action (SUPA, the New Left organization in Canada), wrote an article in which she drew an analogy between the condition of women and that of blacks in North America. She went on to attack penis envy as a myth of the masters. Heather begins the struggle for a separate women's movement:

> Women should undergo this process of self-examination with each other, but away from men . . . women must fortify themselves against the punishment of the male chauvinist and the paternalism of the male liberal. Once women have shared the process of self-discovery and the experience of independent decision-making, they are ready for the real struggle. . . . This is not a struggle against men. . . . Women cannot be free until men are free. . . . The solutions for women lie in solving far-ranging social problems. But this involves nothing short of revolutionary restructuring of the most basic institutions in society . . .[3]

Slowly, women began to follow this advice. We began to talk to each other and to see that what we had considered personal problems were the problems of women. We began to see that

[3] Dean, "On Passing Two Whores and a Nun: The Sexual Caste System," *Random,* October 1966, University of Toronto.

our exclusion corresponded to that of many men who were not aggressive enough to be leaders. Women on community projects realized that they needed a larger movement and that this movement of community organizers excluded them. Men were not consciously excluding us; rather, exclusion stemmed from the collusion of the timidity that women have ingrained in them from a childhood of dolls, and the aggressiveness that men have ingrained in them from their earliest admonishments to "be a man, don't cry." We began to realize that such attitudes are not inherent, but learned. We began to unlearn them.

We began—rather timidly (for we did not want to hurt the fragile movement by showing dissention in the ranks)—to form Feminine Caucuses within the various New Left organizations. We had heard the cry of the black movement to deal with our own oppression. We began to throw off the Protestant ethic heritage of assumptions that all women are expected to sacrifice all their lives, and especially in the movement. Women began to work for their own freedom. At the December 1965 SDS conference, the subject of women's role in society and in the movement was openly discussed. Such discussions were heard elsewhere—Southern Students Organizing Committee (SSOC), Southern Conference Educational Fund (SCEF), Southern Christian Leadership Conference (SCLC) and SUPA. Many debates and discussions have also begun among the women of the militant black movements.

The male response (and sometimes the female response) to the Feminine Caucus was often laughter and disbelief. "What do they want?" "She just needs a good screw." "She's a castrating female." The women who were struggling often felt humiliated. We had not had experience in speaking in large groups and could not articulate well, especially when greeted by remarks such as these. We didn't have any set ideology; we had had no experience in such matters. Many of our papers were joint efforts because most of us felt unable to write alone.

Because of the ridicule, we began to depend upon one another, a new experience for many women, for we see each other as rivals for men. We began to meet separately from movement organizations. Often we didn't know that other groups existed in other cities. But we gained strength in our solidarity. Now men would not attack if several of us were around. The women in Toronto threw out the challenge: "Any man living in a relationship of exploitation who speaks of liberation is voicing political lies. . . . We are going to be the typers of letters and distributors of leaflets (hewers of wood and drawers of water) NO LONGER."

The movement was too slow to respond. The ridicule continued. Some men now began to enter their liberal stage and the advice on how to carry out the struggle was almost overwhelming. Paternalism was rampant. We began to call our little groups Women's Liberation and we excluded men from our meetings and actively sought other women from outside the movement. We learned to express ourselves. We also learned that meetings could be humane and participatory. Women's Liberation grew from women in the movement who were in their twenties, white and middle class to include groups of once non-political housewives, women now married to movement men who previously had no politics of their own, college students, and high school students.

During the winter of 1968, some Chicago women began a *Voice of Women's Liberation Movement* newsletter (VWLM). This excellent publication carried articles on various aspects of the woman question, reports on activities around the country, and featured cartoons, reading lists, and other goodies.

On Halloween, the Women's International Terrorist Conspiracy from Hell (WITCH) surfaced from below Wall St. and hexed the stock exchange, driving the prices down. They have also demonstrated at the Miss America contest and some Bridal Fairs, and, in company with some non-WITCH women, have hexed the Chicago Transit Authority, the Playboy Club and Nixon's Inauguration.

At Thanksgiving, 1968, approximately two hundred women met near Chicago for the first national women's liberation conference. Women came from more than thirty cities and groups. We discovered that the feelings of liberation gained in small groups could carry over to a large gathering. From this, women returned and began more activities. The number and size of groups continues to spread. We are attempting the unique task of beginning a movement in which political ideology and one's personal life may be integrated.

Slowly, the movement groups were responding to the challenge. There were women on most major committees. Both the Canadian and American New Left have women in high positions of leadership. SDS passed a resolution on women at its 1968 conference. Women are now speaking at peace demonstrations. SCEF had a women's liberation organizer. Women played an integral role in the University of Chicago sit-in, which arose over the failure to rehire Marlene Dixon, a radical *woman* faculty member. All movement and many underground papers are now carrying articles on and by women.

Women realize that this is tokenism. A few women making it means little. Blatant chauvinism still exists in the movement—recent women speakers at a peace rally were greeted with hoots, laughter and obscenities. All of the conditions of the early sixties still exist. There are still meetings where no women can speak and women are still accused of only thinking what their lovers think. Men tell women who object to woman's condition that there is something wrong with them. Some women do not recognize the problem and either feel that there is no problem or that something is wrong with them personally.

Women's liberation is a revolutionary demand and we must create the revolutionary women's liberation movement to push for these demands. We can be the vanguard of the revolution when we refuse to listen to the men telling us that "women's demands are reformist." It is clear that the only way for radical men to support our revolution is for us to build a strong independent movement, so that no revolution is possible without us. Then, and only then, will they take us seriously. No amount of education will change them as long as they have a power position to preserve.

We haven't come a long way, baby. The first step has been made, but there need to be many more. When the total impetus of women's demands hits this country, the men and especially the men who control this country will wish for the quiet days of the suffragettes to return. Our demands can only be met by overturning most of the existing structures in society. We hope that the men of the left will join us in the struggle by fighting their own battles, and not trying to tell us what to do. Women are awakening. We are beginning to use our brains, and this awakening could be even more earth shattering than the awakening of blacks.

INTAGLIO:
TIMES THEY ARE A CHANGIN' . . .
Betty La Duke

♀

A Broom of One's Own: Notes on the Women's Liberation Program

A Chicago Women's Liberation Song:
—sung to the tune of "Hold the Fort,"
an old union song

From our kitchens we're emerging
Never to return
We'll join together with our sisters
To struggle and to learn

(Chorus)
Hold the fort for we are coming
Sisters now be strong
Side by side we'll battle onward
Victory will come!

We'll break the chains of male oppression
Where they hold us down
We'll fight for women's liberation
The whole wide world around

(Chorus)
In our minds we hold a vision
Of the world we'll build
Where the dreams of every person have
A chance to be fulfilled

(Chorus)
We meet today in freedom's name
To raise our banner high
We'll join our hands in sisterhood
To battle or to die.

By Charlotte Bunch-Weeks 

In the past two years, the women's movement has mushroomed from a sprinkling of groups in major cities to a movement of perhaps 100,000 women in over 400 cities. In Ohio alone there are groups in some thirty cities, from Cleveland to Chillicothe. Regional and local conferences have taken place all over the nation, reflecting an excitement that this is a movement whose time has come.

Perhaps more important than its growth in size, the women's movement* has grown rapidly in self-confidence, analysis, and program over the past three years. My first women's liberation group, which like many consisted of women active in the New Left, spent much of its first months struggling with our own fears and resistances. We were uneasy about whether we should be spending so much time on ourselves, whether our problems were really a common oppression, and whether other women would respond to us. Today, many of us work full-time with women's liberation; we have not resolved all the issues facing us, but we are confident about our priorities. Where once we felt alone, now we do not have enough time, energy, or resources to respond to the growing interest in this movement. Similarly, women everywhere are speaking out boldly—in the church, in senior and junior high schools, in traditional women's organizations, in black liberation groups, in professional associations, in labor unions, and many other places.

Women's liberation has touched off a resurgence of the women's struggle by giving public visibility and common analysis to an uneasiness and hostility that many women feel, but which had been confined until now to the personal sphere and thereby dismissed. Women are responding because, as one sister put it, women's liberation is simply organized rage against real oppression.

Over the past year, our analysis of women's oppression has developed beyond that presented in some of the earlier articles in

* Even its name has been subject to careful scrutiny and change. Some groups now speak of the Female Liberation Movement, to show that all women of all ages are included, not just adults. We have assumed that the term "women" includes all females.

this book. It has become clear that our opposition is not simply a result of chauvinist attitudes but is indeed deeply rooted in all the institutions of our society. Ours is a sexist or male supremacist society which assumes male superiority (and female inferiority) in all its day to day workings, creating a lower status or a caste for women. A woman is assigned to this caste by sex at birth, and it defines the boundaries of her life and the nature of her relationships with those outside her caste: men. The particular boundaries vary in different classes, but in each, women as a caste are at the bottom.

It is clear that capitalism in the U.S.A., as in many societies in the past, benefits from and perpetuates sexist ideologies for its own profit. It exploits us as cheap labor through unpaid work at home and as a threat to other workers in order to prevent strikes and keep wages down. Through the sacred concept of the nuclear family, it isolates women, defines us as secondary to our men (Mrs.), yet assigns us major tasks for maintaining life, keeping up their castles and their egos, raising children, and so on, all without pay. Further, by creating and exploiting sexual and psychological insecurities, profit seekers use our bodies as commodities and manipulate us into a highly profitable (for them) consumer's market.

All women in the United States are thus exploited economically, psychologically, and sexually. The most immediate forms of oppression vary according to class, race, marital status, and age. Working women are most often oppressed by discrimination, degrading work conditions, and special problems, such as child care, that they encounter on the job. Housewives, especially young educated ones, are most frustrated by their dehumanized and trivialized environment. Welfare mothers are concerned with the immediate and daily economic and social pressures placed upon them. Single or divorced women may be fighting against their marginality and society's scorn, especially if they have children. Students encounter both sexual exploitation and society's attempts to train them for their "proper place"; they note that women in hippie and radical groups don't seem to have escaped male supremacy, as they serve as secretaries, cooks, and playmates for the movement.

Beginning with the daily experiences of many different women, we have just begun to probe the complexity and depths of our oppression. No existing explanations or ideologies adequately interpret our lives. We have therefore begun our own study of sexism, as it relates to other oppressions such as racism and as it works in various socio-economic systems of the past and present. A more comprehensive analysis will grow out of our practical experiences and reflections as we struggle together and separately for our common liberation.

In this struggle, separations that have frustrated previous movements—separations between analysis and program and between personal and political life—are breaking down. Ending sexism means destroying oppressive institutions and ideologies and creating new structures and images to replace them. There is no private domain of a person's life that is not political and there is no political issue that is not ultimately personal. For example, a man who states that he supports women's liberation, but whose relationship to his secretary is oppressive, is politically a male supremacist, regardless of his rhetoric. A woman who has seen the care of her children as her personal dilemma discovers that her response to this situation is basically a political one.

As the women's liberation movement has grown rapidly in size, self-confidence, and analysis, so also it has grown in the development of program. Our programs must both confront the sexist system and enable us as women to struggle for our liberation. This involves three interlocking and reinforcing processes that must go on at once: raising consciousness, ending dependencies, and challenging sexist institutions.

Raising Consciousness

The task of the small group is labeled "consciousness-raising" and refers to a long and logical process which leads to a synthesis of the personal consciousness to which the psychoanalysts have given their attention and the political or class consciousness of the Marxists. . . .

If a woman has reached the point of getting stronger, going out and testing her new role in the world and then getting smashed, her understanding of her oppression is deeper than it was before she got smashed the second time around. She begins to understand that the process of consciousness-raising is in fact a process that probably has no end, that she may now understand the need for collective revolutionary solutions, but her own consciousness is still on the move and she knows not where it will end.

LYNN O'CONNER, SAN FRANCISCO
WOMEN'S LIBERATION
"DEFINING REALITY" IN PAMPHLET *"THE SMALL GROUP"*

Consciousness-raising is our term for the process by which women begin to discover ourselves as an oppressed people and struggle against the effects of male supremacy on us. It happens when we describe and share our individual problems so that we can understand the universality of our oppression and analyze its social roots. It is learning to take pride and delight in our femaleness, rejecting the need to follow the feminine mystique or to copy men as our models; it is learning to trust and love each other as sisters, not competitors for male approval. It is deciding and re-deciding each day, individually and together, that we will take control over our lives, create and support each other in alternative ways of living, and struggle together for the liberation of all women.

A major goal of consciousness-raising, ending our isolation from each other and our silence about the fears and frustrations of our lives, is primarily accomplished through the small group. Pam Allen has described the process of her small group in San Francisco in four stages. First is *opening up*—each individual talks about her feelings about herself and her life, about why she came to a woman's group. Next is *sharing*—the group members teach each other through sharing experiences and build a collage of similar experiences among the women present. The third stage is *analyzing*—the group examines the reasons for and causes of the oppression of women, looking not only at their shared experiences but also at experiences of women in other situations in an effort to gain a sense of the whole. Finally, the group begins *abstracting*—the group removes itself from immediate necessity, takes the concepts and analysis it has developed and discusses abstract theory, drawing on the work of others as well.

While the small group is the most intensive process of consciousness-raising, it is clearly not the only method. Consciousness-raising includes all those ways in which women are brought to see their oppression as a group and are confronted with the question of what they will do about it. Susan B. Anthony stated it clearly in 1872:

> I do pray, and that most earnestly and constantly, for some terrific shock to startle the women of the nation into a self-respect which will compel them to see the absolute degradation of their present position; which will compel them to break their yoke of bondage and give them faith in themselves; which will make them proclaim their allegiance to women first. . . . The fact is, women are in chains, and their servitude is all the more debasing because they do not realize it. O to compel them to see and feel and to give them the courage and the conscience to speak and act for their own freedom, though they face the scorn and contempt of all the world for doing it!

Many women's liberation activities, such as protests at Bridal Fairs and beauty contests, are created to produce that first shock. A WITCH leaflet at a Bridal Fair in New York proclaimed to young engaged women, "Always a Bride, Never a Person." Less shocking but equally important, most groups have courses and forums for new people dealing with all aspects of women's oppression. Courses range in size from 5 to 200, are taught everywhere from junior high schools to community YWCA's, and cover a wide variety of topics.

Increasingly important are women's liberation plays, like "How to Make a Woman," produced in Boston, and media productions, such as "Look Out Girlie, Woman's Liberation is Gonna Get Your Mama," an introductory slide and tape show prepared by Oberlin women. Skits, comic books, pamphlets, tapes, stickers that read "this exploits women" or "this woman is not for sale" to put on ads, newspapers, song books, journals are appearing everywhere. These startle women into a new awareness of their situation and introduce them to the movement for liberation.

But consciousness-raising is not simply awakening to one's condition. It must also be the process of finding the courage and confidence to move. Central to this process, then, is the development of a positive self-image for ourselves as women. Because we have been taught that men are superior and not so limited, most women, especially those who strive to "get ahead," look up to and identify with men, resulting in a dislike of other women and a hatred of ourselves as women. In order to change this self-image, groups can encourage each woman to develop a fuller sense of herself, helping her to take the time and energy to pursue her own identity and interests, and pushing her to develop previously thwarted talents and abilities. Through sharing and working together on projects and in discussion groups, women begin to see each other not as competitors or inferior companions but as sisters in a common struggle who can and must be loved and trusted.

> Our history has been stolen from us.
> Our heroes died in childbirth, from peritonitis,
> —of overwork
> —of oppression
> —of bottled-up rage
> Our geniuses were never taught to read or write
> We must invent a past adequate to our ambitions.
> We must create a future adequate to our needs.
> *THE OLD MOLE,* CAMBRIDGE, MASSACHUSETTS

As part of developing a new self-image, women are discovering the past history of women's struggles for freedom and self-expression. In Cleveland, women held a woman's culture evening, featuring our little-known artists; former suffragettes in Nashville are leading history seminars; women in Chicago and Washington, D.C. have written skits based on our past. Articles and journals are being written, courses taught, and our common history is coming alive again. As part of this consciousness, women held a variety of actions on March 8, 1970, International Women's Day, in honor of a women's strike in New York on March 8, 1908.

Consciousness-raising is not a mechanical act performed in any one way. It is an unending process for discovering ourselves as a group and making ourselves anew, both individually and as a movement, a process that permeates all women's liberation activities. In consciousness-raising we confront ourselves and every woman with our lives, offering alternative visions of what we might struggle to become and opportunities to begin that struggle as part of a group, and we demand that each woman make a conscious decision about her future and the future of her daughters.

Ending Dependencies

Letter to the Cleveland *Plain Dealer:*

In the article about Karen Sue Beineman, the latest Michigan co-ed slain, I notice that in response to her death Eastern Michigan University is now probably going to institute a policy of signing out in the coeds' dorms.

Miss Beineman died because she was strangled. It would have done her little good for the university to know where the kidnapped young woman had been planning to go. Miss Beineman's tragedy was that she, like most women, knew no self-defense. A knowledge of judo or karate might very well have enabled her to break the hold her assailant had on her, deal him a blow that stunned, and run.

It is frightening to think that in our sick society women particularly must fear for their bodies and lives as they go about everyday activities. But it is presently a fact, and so I appeal to women to learn at least the elements of self-defense.

NITA RATNER
CLEVELAND WOMEN'S LIBERATION MOVEMENT

We have all grown up in a male supremacist society that has made us dependent on men and caused us to neglect our growth in many ways: physically, politically, economically, and psychologically. The struggle before us requires that we begin to end these dependencies.

Most of us are afraid of men. We are out of shape and underdeveloped physically, and we do not have a sense of control over our bodies. Women's groups have therefore begun physical development and self-defense courses. On campuses, women are demanding these from the university. At the University of California, Berkeley, women invaded an all-male karate class, chanting, "Open it up or we'll shut it down—self-defense for women!" They charged discrimination since there was no class that women could attend. The result of these activities is both physical and psychological. New York women wrote of their class:

> As a result of karate, we are gaining confidence in our bodies and going through some fantastic changes in terms of our feelings of self-worth. Our confidence has increased not only in confrontations with "dirty-old-men" in the streets, but in non-physical confrontations with our own men and society in general. We do feel as though we have more control over our own lives because of our new potential physical power.
>
> "KARATE AS SELF-DEFENSE FOR WOMEN,"
> SUSAN PASCALE, RACHEL MOON, LESLIE B. TANNER,
> *WOMEN: A JOURNAL OF LIBERATION*

A major dependency common to all women is lack of direct control over the process of reproduction in our bodies. Almost every city now has an abortion counseling and/or birth control information center related to women's liberation. The newly formed center in Minneapolis states their purposes:

> The Woman's Counseling Service deals with the problems of insufficient medical facilities—antiquated abortion laws, inadequate dissemination of birth control, and the lack of readily available medical care—in two ways. Most women have very little knowledge of the medical services available to them; therefore, one function of the Women's Counseling Service is to direct women to those services available to them in the areas of birth control, maternity care, child care, services for unwed mothers, adoption agencies, and venereal disease. . . . The Women's Counseling Service is a place where women can come and talk with trained counselors who are well informed of the "ins and outs" of different agencies, who can talk with women about the fears that they have, and who can give women the personal care and information that is lacking in most public agencies. A very important aim of the Women's Counseling Service is to create a solidarity between women which recognizes that the problems of each individual are the problems of all women—that our "personal

problems" are political, exemplifying the status of women in our society.

What began as counseling and work to repeal abortion laws has expanded into a major emphasis on health care. Women are dependent on a white male medical establishment, not only for abortions, but for all our own care and that of our families. In many cities, women are challenging hospitals, doctors, and drug companies on their sexist, racist, and profit-making assumptions and demanding free and adequate health care for all, not just the rich and privileged.

Courses in mechanics and auto maintenance make women less intimidated by machines and technology. This increases our ability to provide for ourselves and to protect ourselves from fraud at the hands of various servicemen who assume we are ignorant suckers, especially when we are living or traveling alone. *Off Our Backs,* the Washington, D.C. women's newspaper, has a survival column that covers such fundamentals as how to change a tire.

Many women feel intellectually inferior to and politically dependent on men, since we have had little training or experience in political analysis, writing, public speaking, or leading meetings. Women's groups are experimenting with ways to discipline ourselves to overcome these inadequacies, while avoiding the authoritarian political styles of men. Most groups have role playing and discussion sessions that develop every woman's ability to participate in a variety of political activities. Women in Seattle ran a six-week training workshop in public speaking; many groups are also experimenting with new styles that allow more group participation, like skits. Regular political education and strategy sessions also push women to take their intellectual work more seriously.

Psychologically, most women are still very dependent on men. We have real emotional needs for love, praise, comfort, approval, which we have been taught to fulfill through men, rather than through self-confidence and relationships with our sisters. This dependency on men can only be overcome as part of the total process of liberation, as we develop more skills, more self-confidence, and more ability to support each other in these needs. The small groups and some women's collectives have begun this job. From another angle, some seminary women plan to do women's liberation counseling addressed to this need and are demanding that the church provide them with resources.

Some groups have begun to tackle the problem of women's economic dependence on men by pooling their resources, sharing the burdens of housework, and helping each other to find good jobs. The problem of economic dependence can only be solved when we force society to pay us for the work we do in the home and to provide us equal job opportunities and pay outside. In the meantime, various communal and cooperative provisions for doing daily tasks, such as cooking and child care, help alleviate financial burdens and give women more time for other activities.

There are many other needs that women must fulfill in order to function more independently and effectively. Groups are beginning to respond to these through setting up women's houses and centers. A center in the San Francisco Bay area is scheduled to provide:

1. Informational and referral services:
   Employment counseling
   Medical and psychological referrals
   Legal referrals
   Child care facilities
   Educational counseling
   Housing information
2. Library and research facilities
3. Educational programs and a speakers' bureau
4. Communications center
5. "Free space" for women who need someplace to go and be.

While many of these services and activities are aimed primarily at individual needs, they are needs created by our common oppression which must be met for us to work together. As women's liberation encounters more ridicule and resistance, such training and serious networks of support will become even more essential. We must stay alive and grow in order to end the sexist system that has caused our dependencies and to create a liberated people in the future.

Challenging Sexist Institutions

WITCH knows our suppressed history:
that women who rebel are not only
jailed, napalmed, & beaten,
but also
raped, branded & burned at the stake.

We women are:
in jail at Niantic
in the mud of Vietnam
in the slums of the cities
in the ghetto-sinks of suburbia
at the typewriters
of the corporations
at the mimeograph machines
of the Left
in the water at Chappaquiddick
in the brutalizing beds of Babylon

We are going to stop
all confinement of women.

WITCH calls down destruction
on Babylon.
Oppressors:
the curse of women is on you.

HEX FROM WOMEN'S LIBERATION DEMONSTRATION
TO FREE PANTHER SISTERS IN JAIL.
NEW HAVEN, CONNECTICUT

The third essential process involved in the struggle for liberation is confronting both the institutions that oppress us as women and the sexist ideology that supports those institutions. The first women's liberation actions at beauty contests and around the media focused primarily on the ideology—the images of femaleness and their perpetuation in our society. Over the past year women's groups have also begun to analyze institutional oppression, demanding change in those that perpetrate and profit from sexism, such as corporations and the health system. In the process, we have begun to define social structures for a humane, non-racist, non-sexist society, thereby projecting visions for the future and creating what we can now, where that is possible.

No single list of programatic demands and projects has been agreed upon across the country. However, in addition to those activities mentioned in the two sections above, the following are some of the major areas of work: employment/civil rights; abortion/health; media; education; the family/child care.

Employment/Civil Rights

The department, to begin with, was situated like a harem. . . . Women were isolated in one corner of the shop, in one department. . . . The "specialness" of our department lay in the fact that the work we did had been recently reclassified by management from heavy work to light work; this is the way management distinguished "men's work" from "women's work." It was apparent that the designation had nothing whatever to do with heaviness or lightness, but only with rate of pay.

OLGA DOMANSKI, "PAGES FROM A SHOP DIARY,"
NOTES ON WOMEN'S LIBERATION, DETROIT, MICHIGAN

Women's groups are involved in a variety of activities centering on employment, demanding equal pay for equal work, job security, equal opportunity in hiring, training, and promotion not only on the job but also in unions and professional associations, day care and maternity leave without loss of pay, and an end to sexual objectification on the job. Some are organizing or supporting unions of women making these demands in places like hospitals, telephone companies, and during the General Electric strike. For example, Detroit Women's Liberation Coalition is supporting a clerical workers' strike at the Fruehauf Trailer Company; the strikers are meeting great resistance since they are among the first clerical workers to organize a union.

Discussions about women's liberation have been initiated among women workers, especially around universities. During the October 15 Moratorium, Bread and Roses, a Boston Women's Liberation group, sent a memo to office workers, calling for a day off for women:

> Students and professors all over the country are getting the day off. . . . there are probably a lot of people like us—women, secretaries, office and clerical workers—who would like to do something Wednesday but we are all afraid. We are afraid of the real power that the boss has over us, and we are afraid that we are alone. . . . So we think people should ask around in the office today and find out how many others would like to do something on Oct. 15.
>
> "MEMO TO OFFICE WORKERS"

Yale Break, a newspaper for and by women, proclaimed a coalition of women employees, wives and students against "male Yale." As one of its first articles states:

> A lot of anger is building up. Yale is an institution run by underpaid female labor—women work in the kitchens, at the brooms, at the typewriters, in the library stacks, and in the homes. Women work at one-third men's wages. Yale is a male dominated institution whose primary function is to produce the future male leaders of the male society.
>
> "BOW DOWN TO THE KINGMAN, DEAR"
> *YALE BREAK*

Another approach is to challenge hiring practices. In Canada, women are attacking the Canadian Manpower Center for its role in perpetuating job discrimination; one of their strategies is to ask that "all women who file a federal income tax return should deduct by either withholding or requesting a refund, that amount of their tax money which will go to supporting Canada Manpower" ("Women against Manpower," *The Pedestal*). Throughout the United States, suits are being brought charging job discrimination. In San Francisco and Pittsburgh, suits ask that the Equal Employment Opportunities Commission enforce the 1964 Civil Rights Act by ending discrimination between male and female in help-wanted ads in newspapers. College women have begun to challenge the policies of placement bureaus on campus.

Free child-care and more humane working conditions are increasingly important job issues. At several hospitals and universities, women have threatened to bring or have brought their children to the work place. On campuses like the University of Washington in Seattle, uniting around the common project of child-care for employees, students and wives has brought student political groups and university staff together for the first time. Women are also demanding changes in the nature and conditions of their work. Women's liberation in Albuquerque picketed a downtown department store in support of a young Mexican woman who was fired for refusing the manager's heavy-handed sexual advances. In Nashville, women protested a Post Office dress code which permitted a committee of men to measure female employees' skirt lengths and to send them home if hems were more than four inches above the knee.

Further, women are demanding that our civil rights be upheld in all matters of law, business, and public services. Women have protested laws that give husbands control of a woman's property, expensive and humiliating divorce proceedings, "men only" restaurants and clubs, and real estate policies that discriminate against single women with children. Some groups are pushing for an Equal Rights Amendment for women. The Congress to Unite Women in New York in November 1969 said, "While the Fourteenth Amendment guarantees equal protection under the law to all persons who are citizens, the Supreme Court has refused to rule on the issue of whether women are persons."

Abortion/Health

Today at noon the moon,
    Symbol of the female,
Rises to eclipse the sun,
    Symbol of the male.
From the Morgue to your door,
    Our mourning echoes long.
You have killed our sisters—
    In hell you belong!

HEX FOR ABORTION DEMONSTRATION IN DETROIT,
THE DAY OF THE ECLIPSE OF THE SUN

Throughout North America, women have changed the tepid debates about abortion reform of two years ago into a hot campaign to repeal all abortion laws—a campaign pursued through the courts, hospitals, and legislatures. One of the most ambitious was a nationally coordinated "war on Ottawa" declared by Canadian women. Beginning on Valentine's Day, 1970, with demonstrations in Vancouver, women planned actions all over the country to culminate on Mother's Day, when thousands of women, some coming in a black hearse cavalcade across the country, gathered in Ottawa to demand an end to abortion laws in Canada.

In the process of challenging abortion laws, women have quickly realized that the issue is more comprehensive. Attempts at abortion reform have shown us the pervasive sexism and racism of the medical establishment. Where abortion laws have been abolished or significantly reformed, abortions are still difficult to obtain and still expensive. One group expressed its discovery of the nature of medical services:

> When we talked about contraception, we found out that we'd all received very haphazard care, that we'd been ignorant about how our bodies worked and about how contraceptives worked, that our visits to doctors and our discussions had often been surrounded by secrecy, embarrassment, and guilt. We had made many visits to doctors and spent a great deal of money yet had received very inadequate, often callous, care and advice. . . . What started out as discussion quickly became anger. We began by treating "Women and Health" as a discussion topic, and now we're considering what kinds of action to initiate.
>
> WOMEN'S LIBERATION HEALTH COLLECTIVE,
> NEW YORK CITY

Through broader alliances around health issues, we have realized that what is a problem for white middle-class women is twice so for poor and black women. They have even worse general health care, *no* access to safe abortions, and they fear forced birth control and sterilization at the hands of the white male medical establishment.

Women's groups have begun to demand more research on such vital concerns as contraception and more adequate public health care for all, including the right of every woman to *total* control over her body, to bear or not to bear children. In Washington, D.C., women have challenged medical and state negligence in dispensing birth control pills and, with the ACLU, have brought a suit against the public hospital for its neglect of women's health needs, including abortion for indigent residents. At Bowling Green College in Ohio, women students are demanding that university health services provide more birth control information and better health services generally.

We have discovered that better sex education, including an end to sex hypocrisy, the double standard, and exploitative "free" sex is essential to our liberation struggle. Handbooks on abortion, birth control, and sex in general have been published by women's groups and distributed widely, especially on campuses. In Bloomington, Indiana, a group took special training with a psychiatrist and has been conducting sex education seminars in women's dormitories. The overwhelming response to these efforts and to women's counseling services indicates the depth and breadth of health as a gut women's issue.

Media

Women's liberation has responded to the power and exploitation of the media today in two basic ways: first, by challenging and cajoling them to change, and second, by taking them over. One major issue is the sexual objectification of women. A group in New Orleans has articulated women's demands:

> We demand that the television, radio, and newspaper industries establish a new code of ethics, removing from advertisements, news shows, and commentaries all discriminatory allusions to females. Serials, cartoons, and stories which feed off the stereotype images of the "empty-headed" woman, the "fickle" woman, the "bitch" and the "happy" housewife armed with the tools of household slavery, must be discontinued. Let's see as many men as women washing the clothes and dishes, cleaning the house (not as a joke, but seriously). Let's see women washing the car and pole-vaulting. People identify with the models portrayed in the news media.
>
> PROGRAM OF THE SOUTHERN FEMALE RIGHTS UNION, NEW ORLEANS, LOUISIANA

The variety of challenges to the media has overlapped with protests against other social institutions that perpetuate the same stereotypes such as beauty contests, Playboy Clubs, women's auxiliaries, and so on. Protest articles, guerrilla theater actions, boycotts, work stoppages within the communications industry itself have all been used to confront the media. Women within the industry have refused to type, write up, or participate in producing programs or stories which they think are exploitative or degrading to women. Women lawyers may bring a suit against a leading advertiser for defamation of character. Other women, refusing to have anything to do with the established press, have begun our own media: newspapers, journals, films, tapes, comic books, and maybe even a radio station.

Women in New York took over the *Ladies' Home Journal* offices and extracted an agreement for a special supplement to be written and edited by women's liberation groups. Underground papers have been attacked by women in many cities. Women on the *RAT,* a major movement paper in New York, took it over, stating:

> The takeover had to happen. It was long overdue. . . . When a woman can walk into the *RAT* office and say to the editor that she'd like to write for the paper, only to be told, "We've got enough female writers, what we need is a secretary to answer the mail and take the phone calls"; when two or three men out of a staff of ten or twelve people can slap together an issue at the last minute in total disregard for any political opinions the rest of the staff might have; when we who work at the paper have no notion of what each other's politics might be—then the paper is about to die of its own diseases. We *RAT* women want to create a revolutionary rebirth out of that death.

Women in San Francisco forced the "movement" men preparing a pornographic magazine, *San Francisco Review of Sex,* to abandon their plans. These are some of the ways in which women's liberation is working to defeat the overwhelming power of the media to distort our news and to poison us with degrading images of ourselves and our sisters.

Education

In my high school they had three curriculums: occupational, business, and college prep. The occupational curriculum had drafting, and several skilled trades courses. Not one single girl had ever been allowed into this curriculum. . . . They simply placed girls in the home economics courses as electives.

ESTER SERRANO, "BAREFOOT AND PREGNANT," *NOTES ON WOMEN'S LIBERATION,* DETROIT, MICHIGAN

The school system is another institution that discriminates against us and shapes our lives by its sex-role indoctrination and tracking. Women's demands on the educational system have two aims. First, equal educational rights must be guaranteed to all women, which means free and equal access and financial aid in all fields, an end to female tracking in courses and counseling services, and an end to discrimination against women for their marital status, children, or pregnancy. Second, sexist bias in curricula must be eliminated, which requires a vigorous program of critically examining the content of education, women's studies at every level, re-writing of textbooks.

These two thrusts are being pursued in many different contexts and at different levels of the school system from the nursery to adult education. In Durham-Chapel Hill, North Carolina, and in Bloomington, Indiana, women are writing non-sexist children's books. Non-sexist education is basic to all child care collectives and other experimental projects as well. High schools are festering with oppressiveness and high school women are organizing around women's liberation issues.

In colleges, women are confronted with academic discrimination, sexist courses, and social limitations. A women's liberation group at the University of Iowa got its impetus from a university sponsored program entitled "Feminine Focus," which was aimed at educating them to the techniques and strategies involved in "being feminine." In San Diego, women asked for four and one-half faculty positions for women's studies, to which a male administrator suggested they get women volunteers from the community.

The social treatment of women in colleges reflects the status of women generally. Hours, dress codes, and housing restrictions, which women have begun to protest, put a woman under the supervision and protection (control) of men. Since she is not at home under her father's care and not yet in the control of her husband, the university must be her "protector." This situation is based on the notion that a woman's only "real" role is that defined in the family, as daughter, wife, and mother.

Family/Child-Care

Much of women's oppression is rooted in the division of work and status in the home and the human relationships and attitudes developed by the nuclear family. Through the family, women's work at home, and hence on the market, has been devaluated, and her economic dependency and isolation increased.

While, for many women, liberation means dividing up those responsibilities in new ways, so that they can get out of the home, women who prefer or must do housework full-time should be paid. Some homemakers in Stockton, California, are organizing themselves into a union of houseworkers to deal with these grievances. Many women are seeking to find ways of sharing monotonous and trivial housework and are demanding that these tasks be industrialized by the society, thus both paying people to do them and reducing the amount of human energies that they require.

While not necessarily advocating a total end to the family for all people, married and single women in women's liberation are involved in various living experiments. Such experiments include all-female communes, group marriages, cooperative houses, and extended families. Social barriers to these should be abolished, relaxing marriage and divorce laws, changing housing policies that prevent or discourage communal living, challenging social attitudes toward "illegitimate" children, unmarried couples, group living and so forth. Only through experimentation can we discover what variety of social units meet different people's needs for love and security, without oppressing women, men, or children.

Regardless of living style, women's liberation views better child care as a basic responsibility of the society. Child care should be free, creative, available 24 hours a day, but non-compulsory, and run by both men and women. The society should provide all children with adequate food, medical care, clothing, and non-sexist toys. Women have begun to demand such services or the space and money to set them up from employers, the government, and other public institutions.

Since these services do not yet exist and many of us do not want our children programed by our present government and industry, women are also setting up our own child care facilities. Forms vary from daytime play groups to cooperatives, communal living, and sharing of all responsibility for all children. Women are also demanding that colleagues within the movement, both male and female, become more responsive to the needs of children and mothers, in meetings, demonstrations, and travel. For example, women demanded that child care facilities and emergency child provisions be set up for the Mobilization against the War on November 15, 1969.

Child care is essential to the liberation of women, but as two women wisely point out, it is more than that:

> Day care is a people's liberation issue. Women, of course, will gain from a good day care program, but in the final analysis women's liberation depends on an entire transformation of society, not just on one institution. However, that one institution, if radically structured, can help obtain that transformation of society. The way children develop is part of that transformation.
>
> LOUISE GROSS & PHYLLIS MACEWAN, "ON DAY CARE," *WOMEN: A JOURNAL OF LIBERATION*

These are some of the ways in which women's liberation groups are building program for raising consciousness, ending dependencies, and challenging sexist institutions. Many other issues and institutions are involved, but it is impossible to cover everything.

While our analysis and program have grown over the past year, we face many important questions for the future. Most women's groups have just begun to struggle with the questions of structure and leadership. We are asking how to have enough structure to build a mass movement, yet not become bogged down in stultifying bureaucracy. We are seeking ways of avoiding our society's cult of leadership; we want solid leadership without creating special elites. We are struggling with how to relate to other movements and organizations that share common concerns. Should we work as caucuses in other organizations? Should we remain independent? Should we form alliances and, if so, around which issues? Many of us feel that we must build a strong, autonomous women's movement, but we have only begun to define what that will mean and how to do it.

Politically, we have many unanswered questions before us. We have grown in our analysis of sexism, but we still do not understand well enough its relation to racism, imperialism, or class structures in our society. We must define more clearly the dynamic forces of our oppression, its roots, its symptoms, and how best it can be conquered. While these political questions can only be answered in our concrete experiences, we must keep them before us at all times.

In building a strong independent women's movement and defining more clearly its political direction, there will be many hard questions and times. Only as we develop sisterhood, develop the consciousness of our own oppression and the ability to love and trust our sisters will we gain the strength to work together to end the dependencies of a male supremist ideology, to challenge our totally dehumanized sexist society, and to lay groundwork for a new society. This is a lifelong struggle which will itself reveal to us the issues and oppressions with which our daughters and sons must wrestle in the future.

rage submerged
in the muck
of history
whispers beneath
this calm-peace
to shout
its existence.
don't you see?
there—
in the smile
that cries (submissiveness hid you
nicely
distorted you.
delicately it wove
a filigree frame
concealing
with its grace
real beauty.
now
your presence is known
together
we shall give birth
violently
for all to see-feel
your-my touch
of wholeness).

BY MARSHA NORRIS
NEW PRAIRIE PRIMER

I. General or Basic Works

*1. de Beauvoir, Simone. *The Second Sex.* Bantam paperback: Originally 1949. Classic treatment of women, biology and history through to present day.

2. Bird, Caroline. *Born Female: The High Cost of Keeping Women Down.* New York: Van Rees Press, 1968. Good summary of women's present status, especially in employment.

3. Coleman, Richard P., Handel, Gerald, and Rainwater, Lee. *Workingman's Wife: Her Personality, World, and Life Style.* New York: Oceana, 1959. A market researcher's depth study of the nation's largest market—25,000,000 working class women.

*4. Friedan, Betty. *The Feminine Mystique.* New York: Norton, 1963 (Dell paperback). Perceptive and early analysis of "feminine" roles of wife and mother since World War II, especially good on media, advertising, popular Freud, and anthropology.

5. Komarovsky, Mirra. *Blue Collar Marriage.* New York: Random House, 1962. Good discussion of family life and role of women in working class.

6. Lifton, Robert Jay (ed.). *The Woman in America. Daedalus,* Spring, 1964, and Boston: Houghton Mifflin, 1965. Provocative collection of diverse essays: see especially Alice Rossi, "Equality Between the Sexes: An Immodest Proposal."

7. Merriam, Eve. *After Nora Slammed the Door. American Women in the 1960's—The Unfinished Revolution.* Cleveland: World Publishing Co., 1958. Creative discussion and poetry about traps and myths of suburban life for women.

*8. Morgan, Robin (ed.). *The Hand that Cradles the Rock.* New York: Random House, 1970. Anthology of recent women's liberation articles covering a variety of issues, education, sex, psychology, etc.

9. Solanas, Valerie. *S.C.U.M. Manifesto.* New York: Olympia Press, 1968. Rationale and program for Society for Cutting Up Men (SCUM) written by woman who shot Andy Warhol.

II. History

*1. Anthony, Susan B.; Harper, I. H.; and Stanton, Elizabeth Cady.

* Most important items

Bibliography

History of Woman Suffrage. Covers 1848-1920's. Six volumes of the letters, documents, and reflections on their struggle by women's suffrage leaders.

2. Beard, Mary. *Women as a Force in History*. New York: Macmillan, 1946. Contrasts conventional myths about women's social role with historical reality.
*3. Flexner, Eleanor. *A Century of Struggle: The Women's Rights Movement in the USA*. Harvard: 1959 (Atheneum paperback). Most complete history of movement through 1920, though weaker on 1900's.
4. Irwin, Inez Haynes. *Up Hill With Banners Flying: The Story of the Woman's Party*. Penobscot, Maine: Traversity Press, 1964. Official history of the 1912-1920 developments of the women's movement, fills in where Flexner leaves off.
5. Kraditor, Aileen S. *Ideas of the Woman Suffrage Movement, 1890-1920*. Columbia University: 1965. Key intellectual history, especially of the split between older suffragists and newer socialists in women's movement.
6. O'Neill, William L. *Everyone Was Brave: The Rise and Fall of Feminism in America*. Chicago: Quadrangle Books, 1969. Explores obstacles to change in women's situation after suffrage was achieved.
7. Wollstonecraft, Mary. *A Vindication of the Rights of Women*. 1792. W. W. Norton, 1967 paperback edition. Fiery eighteenth century critique by a daring Englishwoman.

III. Social Theory

1. Benston, Margaret. "The Political Economy of Women's Liberation," *Monthly Review*, September 1969. Economic analysis of women's work in the family and its social function.
*2. Engels, F. *The Origins of Family, Private Property, and the State*. 1884. New World paperback. Examines the social organization of primitive man, including marriage and the role of women, and relates this to the rise of class society.
3. Flynn, Elizabeth Gurley. *Women's Place in the Fight for a Better World*. New Century, 1947. Prominent socialist leader discusses role of women.
4. Gilman, Charlotte Perkins. *Women and Economics*. 1898. Harper Torchbooks. Lively collection of dominant progressive ideas of her day, as related to women's situation. Also author of numerous other books on children, the home, human work.
5. Mitchell, Juliet. "The Longest Revolution," *New Left Review*, November-December, 1966. Role of women and how it has not been dealt with effectively in history of socialist thought.

*6. Packard, Vance. *The Hidden Persuaders*. New York: Pocket Books, 1957, and *The Waste Makers*. New York: Pocket Books, 1960. Both good on how we get sold "goods" and on the waste of our society. *The Sexual Wilderness: The Contemporary Upheaval in Male-Female Relationships*. New York: David McKay, 1968. Comprehensive survey of present sexual attitudes.
7. Reed, Evelyn. *Problems of Women's Liberation: A Marxist Approach*. New York: Merit Publishers, 1969. Articles on women and the family, myth of female inferiority, and sex and class.
8. Veblen, Thorstein. *The Theory of the Leisure Class*. New York: 1899, Mentor, paperback. Discusses women as vehicles of conspicuous consumption, among the rich.
9. *The Woman Question: Selections from Marx, Engels, Lenin, Stalin*. New York: International Publishers, 1951.

IV. Psychology, Anthropology, and Religion

1. Daly, Mary. *The Church and the Second Sex*. Harper and Row: 1968. Analysis of women's secondary position in church theology and institution.
2. Fanon, Frantz. *Studies in a Dying Colonialism*. New York: Monthly Review Press, 1965. *The Wretched of the Earth*. New York: Grove Press, 1961; and *Black Skins, White Masks*. New York: 1957. Excellent data on psychological and political effects of oppression.
3. Hays, H. R. *The Dangerous Sex: The Myth of Feminine Evil*. Putnam, 1964; Pocket Books, 1965. Examines various institutional and attitudinal forms that man's fear of woman and her body has taken throughout history.
*4. Maccoby, Eleanor (ed.) *The Development of Sex Differences*. Stanford: 1966. Reviews current research on sex differences and points to the great need for new approaches.
*5. Mead, Margaret. *Male and Female: A Study of the Sexes in a Changing World*. New York: Morrow, 1949, and *Sex and Temperament in Three Savage Societies*, 1935. These studies illustrate how primitive and present cultures determine the meaning of sex and roles socially assigned to each.

V. Sexuality

*1. Brecher, Ruth and Edward. *An Analysis of Human Sexual Response*. Signet: 1967. Excellent discussion of female sexuality and orgasm. More readable than the milestone study it discusses, *Human Sexual Response* by William Masters and Virginia Johnson, 1966.

2. Brecher, Edward. *The Sex Researchers*. Boston: Little, Brown & Co., 1969. Survey of major sex research over past century, including chapter on female sex researchers.
3. Greene, Gael. *Sex and the College Girl*. New York: Dial Press, 1964. Thorough analysis made after numerous conversations with college women in the United States.
4. Lydon, Sue. "Understanding Orgasm." *Ramparts Magazine*, December 14-28, 1968. Summary of debate over female orgasm and sexual pleasure and of implications of this debate.
5. "Sex and the Contemporary American Scene." Special issue of *Annals of The American Academy of Political and Social Science*. Vol. 376, March 1968. Essays reflect on basic sex attitudes and problems of our culture; see especially Rosenberg & Bensman, Boyers, and Ferdinand.

VI. Health, Birth Control, and Abortion

1. Health PAC Women's Collective. Collection of papers on abortion, prenatal care and delivery, contraception, birth control and population control, and day care. In *Health PAC Bulletin* and available from Women-Health PAC, 17 Murray St., New York, New York 10007.
2. Lader, Lawrence. *Abortion*. New York: Bobbs-Merrill, 1966. Very readable general discussion of issue.
3. McGill Students Society. *Birth Control Handbook*. Montreal: 1969. Excellent survey of birth control information, especially aimed at campus. Order from McGill College or Hogtown Press listed below.
4. Maginnis, Patricia T. and Phelan, Lana Clarke. *The Abortion Handbook for Responsible Women*. Contact Books, Inc., 6340 Coldwater Canyon, North Hollywood, California, 1969. Statement of existing situation and how to survive in it; chapters titled, "Qualifying for Rape: Plain Old Rape, Miscegenous Rape, Incest," or "How to Avoid a Neurotic Physician," etc.
5. Washington D.C. Women's Liberation Health Project. Series of papers on women and health, contraception, abortion, excerpts from Senator Nelson's pill hearings and women's pill hearings and questionnaires, etc. Available from D.C. Women's Liberation, Box 13098, "T" Street, Washington, D.C. 20009.

VII. Science and Law

*1. Kanowitz, Leo. *Women and the Law: The Unfinished Revolution*. Albuquerque: University of New Mexico Press, 1969. Discusses inequity to women in abortion, rape, employment, property rights, etc.

2. Mattfeld, Jacquelyn A., and Van Aken, Carol G. (eds.). *Women and the Scientific Professions*. M. I. T. Symposium. Boston: M. I. T. Press, 1965. Collection of articles; see especially Bettelheim and Rossi.
3. Pilpel, Harriet, and Zavin, Theodora. *Your Marriage and the Law*. New York: Collier, 1952 (revised 1965). Women's status under present laws.

VIII. Literature

1. Aristophanes. *Lysistrata* (Dudley Fitts translation). Out of sight story of how women decide to use their sexual power.
2. Di Prima, Diane. *Dinners and Nightmares*. Horace Press, 1966. A collection of her searing poetry, all of which reflects women's consciousness.
3. Ibsen, Henrik. *A Doll's House*. Shocking story of a wife who leaves the confinement of her nineteenth-century home. *Ghosts*. Also shocking in frank dealing with venereal disease.

*4. Lessing, Doris. *The Golden Notebook*. 1963. Autobiographical novel of a woman alone with her child in London; her experiences with sex, independence, as a writer, and with the Left. Lessing is also author of numerous other novels and short stories relevant to women.

5. Woolf, Virginia. *A Room of One's Own*. Harcourt, Brace, 1929. Vivid portrayal of woman's situation and her need for economic and social independence.

IX. Regular Journals and Newspapers of the Women's Liberation Movement as of April 1970

Journals:

1. *Aphra*. Feminist literary magazine—stories, poems, plays, criticism. Four issues a year from *Aphra*, Box 355, Springtown, Pennsylvania 18081.
2. *No More Fun and Games: A Journal of Female Liberation*. Three issues so far; published occasionally. 371 Somerville Ave., Somerville, Massachusetts 02143.
3. *Up From Under*. Women's magazine, to focus on analysis of

women's position and possibilities for change. 339 Lafayette St., New York, New York 10012.

4. *Women: A Journal of Liberation.* A forum of opinion and expression, centered on a particular focus each issue. Four issues a year. 3011 Guilford Ave., Baltimore, Maryland 21218.

Newspapers:

1. *It Ain't Me Babe.* P.O. Box 6323, Albany, California 94706.
2. *Off Our Backs.* 2318 Ashmead Place N.W., Washington, D.C. 20009.
3. *The Pedestal.* Vancouver Women's Caucus, 307 W. Broadway, Vancouver 10, Canada.
4. *RAT,* Subterranean News. 241 E. 14th St., New York, New York 10003.

X. Other Sources of Materials

1. Berkeley Women's Liberation Basement Press, P.O. Box 6323, Albany, California 94706. Distributes papers from West Coast women's movements.
2. Hogtown Press, 11 Olive Avenue, Toronto 174, Ontario, Canada. Reprints of articles from Canadian women's liberation groups.
3. New England Free Press, 791 Tremont St., Boston, Massachusetts 02138. Reprints of numerous women's liberation articles.
4. National Organization for Women (NOW), 509 Fifth Ave., New York, New York 10017. Particularly good for work on education and employment.
5. Society for Humane Abortion, P.O. Box 1867, San Francisco, California 94101. Newsletter and reprints of articles about abortion.
6. United Nations at U.N. Plaza, New York City or UNESCO headquarters in Paris. Numerous statistical documents about women around the world.
7. *Women: A Bibliography,* c/o Cisler, 102 West 80th St., New York New York 10024. Detailed bibliography available for 25¢ and to which this list is indebted.
8. Women's Bureau, U.S. Department of Labor, Washington, D.C. Numerous publications, especially about women workers. Leaflet #10 lists their entire stock.

Cynthia Ozick

—is expecting the paperback edition of her novel, *Trust* (first published by the New American Library in 1966), on May 15. Her poems, translations, fiction, essays, critical essays and reviews have appeared in numerous periodicals, including *Commentary, Midstream, Mademoiselle, Hudson Review* and *Evergreen Review* ("before it became what it is today").

Marlene Dixon

—was the center of a University of Chicago controversy, focusing on women's issues, when she was fired as assistant professor in sociology and human development in the spring of 1969. She has written several articles about women's liberation and is now a professor at McGill College in Canada.

Frances M. Beal

—has worked with the SNCC Women's Liberation Committee, for whom she originally wrote this article. She is presently with the Black Women's Alliance in New York City.

Susan Sutheim

—is news editor for the *Guardian*. A former regional staff member for New York SDS, she is active in women's liberation work there. She's the one who often does "A Word From Our Sponsor" in the *Guardian*.

Marilyn Salzman Webb

—has been active in women's liberation in Washington, D.C. since its beginning and has written numerous articles in the *Guardian* and elsewhere about the movement. At present she works with *Off Our Backs,* a women's liberation newspaper in Washington, D.C.

Del Martin and Phyllis Lyon

—are two of the founders of the Daughters of Bilitis, Inc., a Lesbian organization founded in San Francisco in 1955. At present they are both Board Members of The Council on Religion and the Homosexual, Inc. Mrs. Martin is chairman of Citizens Alert, a group working on the problems of police-community relations in San Francisco. Miss Lyon is assistant director of the National Sex and Drug Forum, a service of

Contributors

The Glide Foundation which seeks to make available to professional persons the most current and reliable information on human sexuality and mind-altering drug use and abuse through an educational format, using a multimedia approach.

Linda Seese

—is a member of the Women's Radical Action Project (WRAP) in Chicago. She was a civil rights worker in Mississippi, Alabama and Columbus, Ohio. She worked on a Student Union for Peace Action (SUPA) Indian project in northern Saskatchewan and was later elected chairwoman of the New Left Committee (NLC), successor to SUPA. She co-authored "Sisters, Brothers, Lovers, . . . Listen" and was a co-founder of the Women's Liberation Movement in Toronto.

Andy Hawley

—is an assistant professor of literature at Massachusetts Institute of Technology. He is the husband of Nancy Hawley, who is active in the Cambridge women's liberation group.

W.I.T.C.H.

—asked to be credited collectively—"just WITCH, because we do it together, you know?" But we can tell you that it was done in New York.

Naomi Weisstein

—teaches psychology at Loyola College at the University of Chicago. She was active in CORE in New Haven and in SDS in Chicago, and she has been involved in "woman's stuff" since 1967. She's currently helping organize an all-woman rock band "to combat the hegemony of chauvinist and oppressive lyrics now in rock." So far they have a flute, a piano, a washpan "and maybe a guitar." She's 29.

Charlotte Bunch-Weeks

—has been active in women's liberation in Cleveland and in Washington, D.C. and helped to organize the first national women's liberation conference in November 1968. She presently works with a collective of D.C. Women's Liberation.

POETS

Diane Di Prima

—is a well-known American poet. The poem included here is from *Revolutionary Letters,* a sequence of poems she has been circulating freely (with permission for anyone to use as they see fit) in generous scorn of property-oriented copyright laws.

Marge Piercy's

—first book of poetry was published by Wesleyan University Press in 1968 *(Breaking Camp);* they will publish her second, *Hard Loving,* in September. Her first novel, *Going Down Fast,* will be published this fall by Trident (Simon & Schuster). Her poems have appeared in many magazines and anthologies. She lives in New York City, is active in the New Left, and is especially involved in Women's Liberation.

Leah Fritz

—describes herself as a "verbal terrorist" who has been "freaking out" the over- and underground press in New York. She has published in *The Village Voice, Liberation* and *The New York Free Press;* is active in the drive for community control of schools, and in the Women's Liberation Movement. "The Playground" is a section of "The Swindle," a long prose-poem about the class structure in Manhattan.

Jean Tepperman

—is a young poet who lives in Dorchester, Massachusetts, and is active in the Women's Liberation Movement.